Easy Programming for the BBC Micro

Easy Programming for the BBC Micro

Eric Deeson
Science Department, Highgate School, Birmingham

Shiva Publishing Limited

SHIVA PUBLISHING LIMITED
4 Church Lane, Nantwich, Cheshire CW5 5RQ, England

ISBN 0 906812 21 6

Cover photograph of the BBC Micro courtesy of Acorn Computers.

Typeset and printed by Devon Print Group, Exeter

Contents

Introduction

This book is explicitly a beginner's guide to working with the marvellous BBC micro-computer. I have therefore done my best to keep its style light while trying to explain what can be quite complex concepts. Whether you are using the book at home or at school, I hope that you will enjoy working with it, and thus enjoy all the time you spend at the keyboard.

The BBC micro, whether Model A or Model B (and I've written throughout for Model A) *is* a marvellous machine. The marvel lies in the huge range of powerful facilities offered for such a low price.

The problem with it is that it is designed to expand with your needs and with future developments. In order to cater for that expansion, programming it often seems un-necessarily difficult. You will feel that, whether you are quite new to computing or have gained much experience with other micros, cheap or costly.

A number of people have observed that the Beeb is not a beginner's machine. They say that because of this complexity in its BASIC language. Yet experts with other micros have to struggle with the BBC machine too, even if they agree the struggle's worthwhile. So I've written this to help minimize *your* struggles. While the struggle *is* worthwhile, it can't be bad to minimize the agony. Enjoy this book—it represents a huge number of struggles on my part—and enjoy and value your BBC micro.

This book was written before the BBC *Manual* had appeared and before more than a handful of books and magazine articles. I must express my gratitude to John Coll of Acorn Computers who offered to try to answer all my questions. I also gained much of value from many personal discussions and from:

> *BASIC Programming on the BBC Micro* by Neil Cryer (Prentice/Hall)
> *BEEBUG Newsletter*
> Articles in *Your Computer* and *Popular Computing Weekly*.

Allow me to express my gratitude also to Rita Wagh who faced, without protest, the awesome task of typing, and AVC Software who kindly permitted me to use some ideas from my book *Learning with the Beeb*. My family showed their usual patience as I closed myself in the spare room for hours on end sweating over a hot keyboard.

Soon enough there will be plenty of books on the Beeb. Use this one in conjunction with the *Manual* and programs in the personal computing magazines. When you've finished it, I hope it will remain of permanent value for reference, even when you've graduated to a book on advanced BBC programming.

Birmingham, June 1982   Eric Deeson

DEDICATION

This book, and all the struggles it represents, are dedicated to my son Richard, an enthusiastic user of the machine from the day it arrived.

Note: A box □ is used to represent a space when one is not otherwise obviously needed.

1 Getting Stuck In

You would be a most unusual person if you were reading this before getting your BBC micro-computer out of its box and seeing if it works. But we must cater for all tastes . . . Anyway, you may have tried to get going without our help and have come across some problem. So, right from the postman's knock, here's how to get stuck in to your Beeb.

PREPARATION

Prepare your working site You're going to need a TV set, so push the little ones out of the way. You're going to need a power point near the TV, so if necessary get an adaptor (yes, safe enough if your system is a 13 A ring main). You're going to need a low table for the equipment—clear off the beer glasses and old newspapers and put it a metre or so in front of the TV. You're going to need a comfortable seat at that low table. Our kids have got one of those enormous bean-bags—I have priority on that.

If your micro-computer works, and you like using it, prepare yourself for many hours a week at the keyboard. At the end of this section, I'll come back to a proper working site—the above is temporary, but a lot better than working on the floor.

Prepare the computer This is what you should have in the box. Keep it all in there when not in use. For one thing, bits can be lost, damaged, or attacked by children and other household pets if left lying around. For another, computing needs a tidy mind, so we'll start right now. (For another, you may just need to send the computer back; it'll cost you a packet in packaging if you can't find the original stuff.)

I'll start again. This is what you should have in the box:

1. The polystyrene foam container. Find out which half is the top and mark it TOP. That's going to save accidents later.
2. The computer itself. That's the big typewriter thing. It has its own 13 A plug already—that saves the usual hassle of initiating new electric equipment, but does mean you can't run it with the tape recorder off one plug. Be careful when lifting the machine; it's fairly heavy and the top flexes a bit.
3. The video lead. That's the long black one. (Black is a bad colour for most of us—hard to see, so easy to trip over.)
4. The audio lead. That's the short grey one with bare wires at one end. You're right—there'll be problems there.
5. The *User Guide*. By the time you read this, there should be a proper manual. At the time I write this, there aren't even any proofs of that, so I can't give page references.
6. A paperback sized box saying "Welcome" in all the colours of the Spectrum. Inside it, an audio cassette and a booklet, both saying "Welcome" again.

Try to remember where the bits come from. You're going to put them all neatly back again, right?

The box should by now be empty. If it isn't, your next action depends on what there is, and how technical you are. If there are odd washers etc. and there's a rattle in the computer's case, you ought to investigate. The rattle may be a metal screw which could short-circuit something. If there are odd key-tops floating around, try to replace them, with care and firmness.

Anything else, you're best advised to get in touch with the supplier. Don't forget that messing around inside the micro may not only fail—but could invalidate the guarantee.

Don't be put off! Chances are that there'll be no problems at all. Anyway it's not my job to write a maintenance manual.

GETTING IT TOGETHER

1. Plug in the computer; switch on at the socket; switch on at the back of the box. The micro should bleep at you and the "caps lock" light at the left side of the keyboard should come on. The Beeb's speaker may buzz; it shouldn't, but ignore it unless it's really annoying.
2. Switch on the telly. Don't be distracted by the picture. It's what the little ones were watching before you turfed them out.
    To get *your* picture:
    (a) Connect the video lead between the "UHF out" socket at the back of the micro (do it properly; it's a tight fit) and the TV's aerial socket. (You *must* use a UHF TV, not an ancient VHF one or a less ancient dual-standard set.)
    (b) Select a spare channel on the TV; tough if you watch four channels and have only four switches—use the least popular channel then. You will now see multi-coloured or black and white "snow" on the screen. Depends whether it's a colour or monochrome set you're using.
    (c) Slowly tune the channel's adjuster knob until you get the clear message:

    > BBC Computer 16K (or 32K for Model B)
    > BASIC
    > > _   (that dash flashes on and off; the two symbols are cursors, or
    >   *prompts*)

    The tuning position is close to the broadcast channels, and very close to that for Acorn Atom, Sinclair ZX81 or Spectrum if you've been using any of those micros before.
3. Turn the TV sound right down. You won't need it while using this book.
4. Type in the following commands. This is where you start learning your way round the keyboard. After each command press the RETURN key; I've coded that (R) here.

MODE 5 (R)	[top two lines of message vanish; rest changes scale]
COLOUR 129 (R)	[your command appears in white; prompts move down]
CLS (R)	[screen clears to red or grey, + prompts]
PRINT "HALLO"	[use SHIFT key and 2 together to get " "]
(R)	[your message appears below the command]

You can play with those commands if you like. I put them in so you could get something on screen to adjust the TV controls. Do that—to get the best picture you can. Adjust whatever your set allows—colour, brightness, contrast, channel tuning, holds. Get the best picture you can; don't worry about the little ones' *Blue Peter*.

If any of this doesn't work and the TV was all right before, either there's something wrong with your power supply (not even step 1 got you anywhere) or with the computer. The latter's not likely really . . .

"WELCOME"

BBC Soft have done a lot of work for me in preparing this cassette. Now's the time to use it. Problem: the bare wires on the end of the audio lead. You're going to have to experiment to find out how to connect your cassette recorder to the "cassette" socket at the back of the micro. Try any audio leads you may have in your house—you may be in luck. Otherwise you're going to have to spend time and money getting a suitable lead by post or from a local audio shop. Refer to pages 10 and 11 of the "Welcome" booklet.

Spend a couple of hours on the "Welcome" tape, following the excellent booklet. That will give you lots of ideas about what micros can do, and will give you keyboard practice too. You're not going to get far into using a computer before you'll be needing the cassette recorder a lot—so just as well get it sorted out now.

Meanwhile, a bit of theory before we go on.

You got the machine to do various things earlier by giving it *commands*. Each had to be completed by pressing the RETURN key (R). This tells the computer that you have finished and it's its turn to do something. There's no way you can get the computer to do a load of things fast by giving it a series of commands. What we do instead is to *program* the computer. This means giving it a collection of commands (now called instructions or *statements*); the computer stores these and carries them out when you want.

This computer cannot keep programs stored when it's switched off, so it has the facility to SAVE them on cassette (or in other ways). The "Welcome" cassette has a series of such recorded programs; by the time you've finished this book, you'll have a series of recorded cassettes of your own, each available for use when you want it.

And after the theory, a *warning*. When you've worked through this book, you'll be a fairly good programmer. But you *won't* be able to produce programs like some of the more sophisticated ones on the "Welcome" cassette. That requires a great understanding of computers and a great experience of advanced programming. And months of hard work sweating at the keyboard.

What I can, and shall, do is at the end of the book give you pointers to where you *can* find out more. This book, with the *Manual* for reference, is only the first step to fame and fortune as a maker of BBC programs. So, let's get on with programming . . . Oops, I nearly forgot. I said I'd come back to a permanent computer user's corner.

FIXTURES

Using a computer is a marvellous hobby. But as with all hobbies, it needs a bit of effort to fix things up right. You can't hog the TV set for ever. You can't work for long on a bean-bag. So once you're sure you're going to enjoy computing (if you're not sure yet), *organize*. You'll need the items listed overleaf:

1. A table and chair in a quiet corner, with adjacent power, and storage space at hand.
2. A TV set just for this purpose. A black and white portable is OK, but consider a guaranteed second-hand colour set from a local shop. Good ones are available for under £50.
3. A permanent arrangement of everything on the table, allowing you to work quickly and for a long time without strain. I've sketched a suitable layout for your BBC corner (right-handed user) in Figure 1.1. Make sure it's appealing to visitors when you proudly show off your work—but not too appealing for stray infants poking around in your absence. Or parents . . .

Right, *now* can we start into programming?

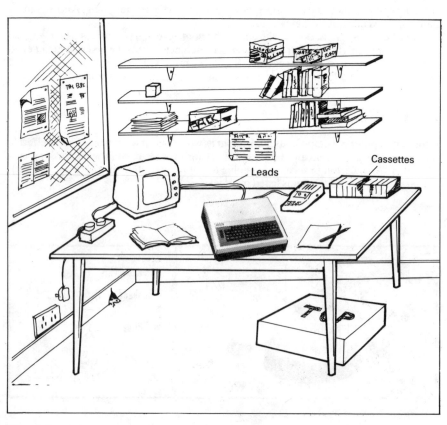

Figure 1.1

2 What is a Computer?

Hold on. I know you're raring to get stuck into using your BBC micro—but first I think you should get to know just a little about it. What *is* a computer?

For a start, there are lots of kinds of computers. You've probably got some of those shown in the picture (Figure 2.1). These are special-purpose computers, *dedicated* to a special task in each case.

The BBC micro is a *general-purpose* computer—with suitable instructions it can do the work of *any* dedicated machine. I hope you've run through the "Welcome" tape by now; there are instructions (programs) in there for timing, calculating and gaming—as for various other tasks.

A general-purpose computer can do many different things if suitably instructed.

DEFINITIONS

Here's the full definition of a computer like the BBC micro:

A computer is a general-purpose, high-speed, digital electronic, stored program data processor.

We've seen what "general-purpose" means. What about the rest of the description?

High-speed An important thing about computers is that, suitably instructed, they can work much faster than people. (They don't get tired or go on strike either; well, not usually.) I'll come back to this point in a few pages—but the modern micro can carry out several million actions in a second. That means it can do complex operations very quickly and keep up with fast changing situations.

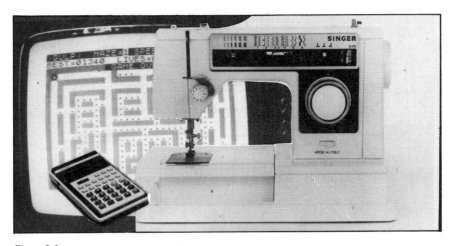

Figure 2.1

Stored program As you know, a program is the name given to a set of instructions for the computer. Now, you think what it would be like giving the computer each instruction in turn, when the computer can carry out millions in a second. Right, the micro would be sitting around 99.999% of the time twiddling its electrons while the human operator's getting round to the next instruction. That would be a great waste of the machine's potential.

Digital electronic That's a bit technical. It means that this is an electronic system, working with tiny electric currents. (Actually it's *micro*-electronic—those currents are *really* tiny.) The "digital" bit refers to the fact that the currents run around in pulses; these can be counted, so they're like numbers. "Digits" means "numbers".

Data processor Is what computing's all about. The computer processes data (representing information of interest to humans) to produce more data (more interesting information). Think how computers are used; think how we use the BBC micro in this book—then you can see why people call computing "data processing".

THE PARTS OF A COMPUTER

No, don't worry—I'm not going to get very technical. But I think it would help if you understand that all digital computers have the same basic structure. This applies to modern tiny pocket computers and it applies to the BBC micro.

The bit that does the hard work is called the *processor*. What does it process?—data. How is it instructed?—by program. Data and programs must be stored. So close to the processor is the memory, or main *store*.

As you learned from "Welcome", we can feed material into the store from cassette (and vice versa). So, connected to the main store is the *back-up store*; in our case this is a cassette recorder and cassettes, but the BBC can also use a system based on magnetic discs.

All computers must be in communication with the user. The user must be able to feed in commands, instructions and data. The *input unit* deals with that need; that's the BBC's keyboard. And the computer must be able to give the user messages and data—it has an *output unit*. The TV screen is the standard micro's output unit. A printer, if available, is another one. The way the bits fit together is shown in Figure 2.2. Note that folk often use the word *peripherals* (= outside parts) for the input/output units and back-up store.

There, that wasn't so hard, was it?

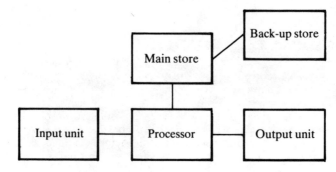

Figure 2.2

3 What is a Program?

I hope you find that a simple question to answer, as we've mentioned it twice already!

A program is a set of instructions (or statements) the computer can follow.

If you want to instruct someone to do something, you must use a language they can follow. Not many of you will (I guess) be able to carry out *these* instructions:

Odkholl. Min fadlak irsil laenae mayya.

As this isn't a BBC Arabic course I won't go further, but I hope you get the point—computers, like people, must be able to comprehend your instructions.

BBC computers are able to comprehend your instructions if they're entered through the keyboard correctly in the BASIC language. The following commands that you've already used are part of that language:

MODE 5   (R)
COLOUR 129   (R)
CLS   (R)
PRINT "HALLO"   (R)

So too is CHAIN "WELCOME" that you used with the "Welcome" tape.

A set of commands is not a program—they must be entered one by one and the computer doesn't remember them. To make a program the commands must have numbers in front of them. We call these *line-numbers*. They have two uses:

1. The line-number tells the micro that the rest is a program instruction, not a command.
2. The order of line-numbers is the order in which the computer must carry out the instructions.

Each program statement must start with a line-number (and end with (R)). The line-number may be any non-negative whole number up to and including 32767.

I don't expect you will ever write a BBC program with 32767 instructions—a good thing, as the machine's memory isn't large enough to hold that many! So I suggest that in your programs you leave plenty of space between line-numbers. I'll stick to line-numbers going up in steps of ten as that is common practice. This has a great advantage anyway—it's easy to insert extra lines if you need.

A SIMPLE PROGRAM

Here's a simple program. Enter it.

     10 MODE 5 (R)   [Note: 0 means zero, not letter "Oh"]

     20 COLOUR 129 (R)

     30 CLS (R)

     40 PRINT "HALLO" (R)

What happens when you've finished entering? *Nothing*. The computer hasn't been commanded to do anything, so it doesn't.

To start a program going, we need another command. It is RUN (R). Try that. Hey presto, it works! You end up with a red screen and the word "HALLO" appearing nicely at the top. Below that message are the two prompts. Type RUN (R) again. I bet you missed what happened! The whole process took place again, but so fast you can hardly notice it. Try it once more—RUN (R). See? The program works every time you enter RUN (R).

So there's a big difference between commands and program statements—the computer has stored the program instructions and carries them out in order whenever you tell it to RUN (R).

Look, I'll do a deal with you. I don't want to keep saying (R) to you each time you need to press RETURN. Can you remember to use RETURN after each program line, after each command, after anything you've finished typing in? In exchange, type in this command exactly as printed:

    KEY 0 "RUN ¦M" (R)   [is shift colon; ¦ is shift with the key below and to
                                the right of the BREAK button]

Now, every time you press the red key marked f0, the program in store will run. And (I hope not to confuse you) this time you don't even need to press RETURN.

So, now you've got a program in store. You can prove it by using RUN (R), or the red f0 key—every time you do, the same thing happens. But you never see the program! Well, that's a good thing to the computer user. He or she doesn't want to be bothered by the instructions. But the programmer *does* want to see what's in store—to change it or check it or just admire it. Use the command LIST. Did anything happen? If not, it's because you forgot (R), didn't you? LIST prints out on screen a copy of the program in memory. Yes, only a copy—it's still there, as you can check with f0.

COMMANDS AND STATEMENTS

We've seen that BBC BASIC commands—MODE 5, COLOUR 129, CLS and PRINT "HALLO"—can be used in programs as instructions. Is that true of them all?

LIST your program and add a new line—50 LIST. RUN that (with f0)—and you get an *error message*—"Syntax error at line 50". Unlike some micros, the Beeb won't accept LIST as a program statement. (That's a pity, actually.)

OK, so try 50 f0. On the screen appears 50 RUN and you don't need (R). Fair enough, as f0 means RUN (R). Now press f0 again, to RUN the program. And you get a pretty pattern. Could watch it for hours? The program starts at the start, reaches 50 RUN, so starts again, and so on. This program can't stop. It'll go on for ever. We're in what the jargonists call a closed loop. Could watch it for hours? We're going to have to.

Fortunately, as closed loops may happen by accident, all micro designers have invented ways of breaking out. That's right, the BREAK key. Try it. The pretty pattern stops, the screen clears and—we're back to square one. The screen looks almost the same as when the micro was switched on. So have we lost the program? LIST—nothing. RUN—nothing. f0—nothing. No, don't fret, we *haven't* lost the program; it's in there somewhere. You can get it back—the command is OLD (= get back the old program we thought was lost). Now LIST—there it is. f0—and off it goes again.

That BREAK OLD (R) routine is a bit of a bind. You've probably noticed the ESCAPE key by now (over on the left). Try that. The program stops with a message referring to a line-number. So there's a program with that line-number. LIST: OK. f0: OK. So ESCAPE is a less drastic process than BREAK.

Personally I prefer BREAK, and as that can be programmed like the red keys next to it, I do so, with OLD and LIST. Like this:

*KEY 10 "OLD ¦ M LIST ¦ M"

A useful trick not many people know about. (The fact that you can program the BREAK key any way you want means that practical jokers can have a lovely time. I'll leave *that* to your imagination, but see if you can program the BREAK key so that it sets the program running again. That can be useful on occasion.)

ANOTHER PROGRAM

Time for something different. This next little program is a fairly weedy guess-the-number game—but I shall use it to discuss some basic BASIC statements. And *you* should use it to explore those statements. Before you start, type NEW to clear the memory, and AUTO to let the computer feed you the line-numbers.

Program 1: Guess the number

10	MODE 5	
20	COLOUR 129	
30	CLS	
40	UNKNOWN = RND (10)	
50	REPEAT	
60	PRINT "Give me a number	[Use CAPS LOCK to give small let-
	between 1 and 10."	ters and note the three extra spaces]
70	INPUT ANSWER	
80	UNTIL ANSWER = UNKNOWN	
90	PRINT "RIGHT"	
100	ESCAPE	[ESCAPE stops the AUTO routine]

Press f0 to RUN (NEW doesn't empty the red keys). Does it work? Run and run again. If the program doesn't work, either I've got to shoot myself for poor proof-reading—or you should shoot yourself for poor typing.

Use BREAK to give you a listing, and follow through the comments overleaf.

11

*MODE (line 10)—the BBC computer offers eight different display modes (see the *Manual*). Only four of these (4, 5, 6 and 7) are available in Model A; of those MODE 5 is the colour mode with large characters. Personally I use it quite often. Try different modes, by entering different line 10s and running them in turn. Compare the effects. If you're in Model A, you'll find only MODE 7 giving effective results—and then not in colour. Get back to 10 MODE 5.

*COLOUR (line 20)—this statement is used to select background colour (in MODE 5: 128 black 129 red 130 yellow 131 white) and foreground (text) colour (0, 1, 2, and 3 correspondingly). Explore the effects of different colour statements in MODE 5 and in the other modes available to you. Note which ones you like best!

*CLS (line 30)—the screen clears to the background colour + prompts.

*UNKNOWN = RND (10) (line 40)—this is an *assignment statement*. It means that the computer must choose at random—RND—a number between 1 and 10 (inclusive) and call it UNKNOWN. If you explore this, remember to change the numbers in line 60 as well. (Thus if you use UNKNOWN = 10 + RND (20) the limits in line 60 would be 11 and 30.) In this kind of assignment statement the name before the = sign (the assignment operator) is called a *numerical variable* (a number that can vary in value). Its value is *assigned* to be the value of the *numerical expression* after the =.

UNKNOWN	=	20 + RND (30)
numerical variable	assignment operator	numerical expression

LOOPS

*REPEAT . . . UNTIL . . . (lines 50 and 80) set up what folks call a loop—the computer is told, by REPEAT, to carry out the next instructions again and again UNTIL something becomes true. I can show best what's happening here with a diagram, Figure 3.1.

Can you see what's happening? Each time through the loop the computer PRINTs on screen the message "Give me a number . . .". It then displays a prompt, the query mark telling the user to do something, and waits till the user types in a number and (R). The computer then assigns the input number to the variable ANSWER and checks whether ANSWER = UNKNOWN or not. If not—round the loop again.

Much of that has of course told you about the INPUT statement. It corresponds in a way to the INPUT part of the computer discussed a few pages back, with PRINT corresponding to the OUTPUT side. INPUT is quite complex. To repeat, INPUT A tells the micro to:

1. Display the prompt "?".
2. Wait for a keyboard input + (R).
3. Print on screen what was input.
4. Assign the input number to the variable A.

And that's pretty well dissected Program 1. If you want to relax a lot, enter and play with the first program (A1) in the set at the end of the book. But try to understand it too!

If you want to relax a little, try some of the projects on page 14.

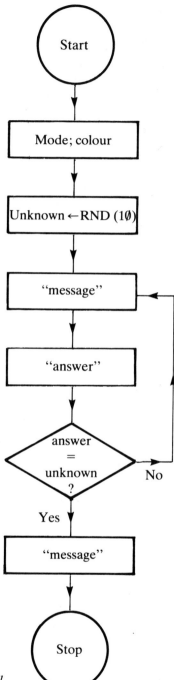

Figure 3.1

13

PROJECTS

1. Adapt Program 1 by each of these stages in turn:
   (a) Let the program re-start automatically each time it's run, UNTIL ANSWER = 0. (0 is called a "rogue value"—one used to stop a loop.)
   (b) Insert 25 COLOUR 2. Then try to arrange things so that background and foreground colours are assigned at random—but never the same (why not?).
   (c) Introduce a line 75 starting IF ANSWER < > UNKNOWN PRINT something suitable. Note that "< >" means "doesn't equal".
   (d) Improve the other PRINT messages.
2. Use the symbols < (is less than) and > (is greater than) with IF and messages as in 1 (c) to give the user clues in Program 1.
3. Add to Program 1 line 45 GUESS = 0 and work out how to count how many guesses the user has had. Then tell him or her.
4. Make up a program of your own using REPEAT/PRINT/INPUT. Make this so good that the rest of your family enjoy running it. Don't forget to NEW first! (Why?)
5. Throughout, get used to the keyboard, and to the red FUNCTION keys (like f0).

4 What Programming is About

This book is *not* a programming text. Sure, I'm trying to help you get into BBC micro programming, but I'm *not* going to spend a lot of ink on telling you what good programming is (even if I knew). When you've finished the book, and perhaps started to think seriously of programming for profit, then *you* must find out what makes a good program.

All the same, there are good habits and bad habits. And if you get into good habits early on, you'll be glad later.

PLANNING

The essence of good habits in programming is *planning*. The worst thing to do with a program idea is to sit down at the keyboard and start typing it in. YOU WILL GET INTO AN AWFUL MESS. And even if, by a miracle, the result works, it will not be very efficient; it may have BUGS in it (dreaded hidden errors); and it will not impress the folk who look at it and use it.

Efficiency in programming means having a product which works correctly in all circumstances, works at the right speed, uses a minimum of memory, and looks good to everyone involved. So your planning must aim for these criteria.

The essence of program planning is a procedure called *top-down development*. This means breaking the initial idea down into smaller and smaller chunks until each one is an easy to handle unit. Actually we use the words *module* or *routine* for those final units. You may be able to get the idea from Figure 14.3 on page 75. That kind of program description is called a *flowchart*, and I'll have more to say about it later. The sketch, Figure 4.1, shows what top-down programming entails. See what I mean? The original broad concept breaks down into a lot of small chunks.

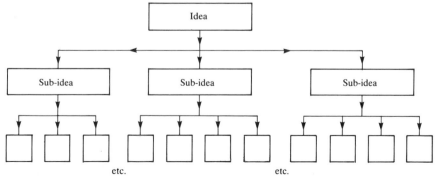

Figure 4.1

Now I'm not going to say that you've got to work out a set of modules for the short programs we're into at the moment. But I do say that you should view your program not as a whole but as a number of separate parts. Each part has its own aim; each part is programmed separately and tested separately. Then the whole thing, made of those parts added together, is likely to be neat, efficient, *and* bug-free.

Another aspect of planning is, as I say, appeal to the user. We say that a program must be *user-friendly*—the user must be kept at ease and never wonder what to do. The most important thing here concerns planning the screen messages. These should be short but clear, well laid out and not cramped together—and *make sure that your spelling and punctuation are correct!* (I'm a teacher and am too often horrified by finding poor grammar in teaching programs—that to me is inexcusable. Some researcher recently pointed out, by the way, that it is better for a programmer to be good at English than good at math's; this is partly why.)

I've already started using large and small letters in screen messages in this book. These are easier to read than capitals alone and also make the screen more interesting. Get to know the CAPS LOCK key therefore. When its light is on, typing a letter gives you the capital (upper case) form; when the CAPS LOCK light is off, you get the lower case except when using SHIFT. Complicated? Practise it.

There is a catch here, though. All the keywords you use—PRINT, LIST, CHAIN, CLS and so on—*must* be in upper case letters (capitals), or the computer won't recognize them. That means you *must* re-press CAPS LOCK after typing in a lower case message. That's a bind, I know—but the result *is* worthwhile.

5 Getting Round the Screen

Surely one of the most versatile BASIC instructions is PRINT, which sends an output to the screen display. We've used it a lot already. In this chapter I want us to go through with care the different ways of using it. We shall look at PRINT instructions to:

1. Produce a nice-looking display.
2. Put your own shapes on screen.
3. Move characters around the screen to give animated displays.

First, I'd like you to BREAK and define f∅ to give RUN (R) and the BREAK key to give BREAK OLD (R) LIST (R) as before. (This assumes you've just switched on.) Then enter, RUN and think about this little program.

1∅	MODE 5	[colour mode]
2∅	COLOUR 129	[red background]
3∅	COLOUR 2	[yellow foreground]
4∅	CLS	[clear screen]
5∅	PRINT "some message or other."	

If you've entered that exactly as shown, you should have (at least) two criticisms about the display. The first is that the message is cramped almost unreadably at the top of the screen. The second is that it appears on the top line except for "r."—the message is broken in the middle of a word because in MODE 5 you can have only twenty characters (numbers, letters, spaces etc.) on a line.

There are many ways of using PRINT, however, some of which will help you get over the first problem. While we're dealing with that, notice how the second problem can be dealt with too.

THE PRINT STATEMENT

Unless the computer is specifically told otherwise, each time it meets a PRINT instruction, it starts a new line. This is true whatever it is going to print, even if it's nothing. So "PRINT nothing" means skip a line. Try it—add line 45 PRINT to your program. Better—yes?

That's one way we can get over our first problem. The second way is to use the TAB function, which is rather like the TABULATE you get on posh typewriters. Remove line 45 by entering 45 (R)—you can check that with LIST—and enter this new version of line 5∅:

    5∅   PRINT TAB (24); "Some message or other."

When you RUN this version of the program—lo and behold, we've got over *both* our display problems. Not only is the message started on the second line, but it is indented so that the last word is no longer broken.

How does TAB (number) work then? What it does is to count off the number of spaces given in the brackets before it starts displaying the message.

Here's a slightly posher PRINT program now. I hope you like it—but its job is to help you understand TAB!

Program 2: A simple name pattern

```
 10   MODE 5
 20   COLOUR 129
 30   COLOUR 3
 40   CLS
 50   PRINT TAB (22); "What is your name";     [note final semi-colon]
 60   INPUT NAME$                              [note final $ sign]
 70   A = 0
 80   REPEAT
 90   PRINT
100   PRINT TAB (A); NAME$                     [note final $ sign]
110   A = A + 1                                [counting]
120   UNTIL A = 10
```

OK, OK, I know it's not brilliant, but we *are* getting on.

Now that program illustrates several points. Here they are.

1. PRINT TAB (number), as in line 50, to start printing at a suitable point on a suitable line.
2. PRINT TAB (variable), as in line 100, to start printing at a point determined by the value of a variable.
3. PRINT nothing, as in line 90, to skip a line.

The program also introduces two new ideas. One is the dollar sign, which I'll come back to in a bit; the other is the semi-colon at the end of line 50.

Now actually that semi-colon is just like the one after each TAB (...)—it tells the computer that the next thing printed is not to go on the next line, but is to follow straight after the last thing. The next thing printed after line 50 is the query mark that appears with line 60 (INPUT)—we've made that go on the end of the message where it really ought to be.

With the use of punctuation marks like the semi-colon, PRINT statements can be very flexible. The next program shows this, and also introduces the apostrophe (')—this tells the computer to go to the next line. (Get apostrophe with SHIFT 7.) NEW before you enter!

Program 3: Address format

```
 10   MODE 5
 20   COLOUR 130
 30   COLOUR 1
 40   CLS
```

```
50   PRINT TAB (22); " What is your name";
60   INPUT NAME$
70   PRINT TAB (22); "And
     your house andstreet";                    [space missed on purpose]
80   INPUT STREET$
90   PRINT TAB (22); "And the place";
100  INPUT PLACE$
110  COLOUR 0
120  CLS
130  PRINT ' ' NAME$ ' ' TAB (2); STREET$ ' ' TAB (4); PLACE$ ' ' ' '
```

The important thing here is line 130. Please make sure you understand exactly how it lays out (formats) the screen display the way it does.

By the way, I've used CLS (= clear screen) about a million times by now. I ought to tell you that it, too is of great value for screen formatting. Clear the screen often, to remove finished-with material, to prevent clutter—to make the display nice and useful.

There's one more PRINT punctuation technique to know about—using the comma. It appears in line 130 of Program 4 (which, as usual, also employs one or two other new ideas!).

Program 4: Tables of squares

```
10   MODE 5
20   COLOUR 128
30   COLOUR 2
40   CLS
50   PRINT ' "Give me a number!"
60   INPUT A
70   PRINT ' ' "Thanks!"
80   CLS
90   PRINT ' TAB (4); "Number"; TAB (14); "Square"
100  B = A
110  REPEAT
120  PRINT
130  PRINT B, B ↑ 2                    [↑, the "power" sign, is on the
                                        second row]
140  B = B + 1
150  UNTIL B = A + 9
```

The comma in micro PRINT statements corresponds to the restricted TABULATE you get on less costly typewriters. In effect the screen display is divided into *zones*, each ten character spaces wide. (So in MODE 5 there are two zones, while most of the others have four.) PRINT, "message" will start the display at the beginning of the second zone. Numbers, on the other hand, appear lined up at the right of the zone used, as you saw with line 130 of Program 4.

STRINGS

Now (at last) I can get back to the bit I was saving, the bit about the symbol $. We first met this in Program 2, where line 6Ø was INPUT NAME$, and whose line 1ØØ was PRINT . . . NAME$.

The symbol $ stands for, and is pronounced, "string". So what's a string? Well, look at that line 6Ø again: INPUT NAME$. We learned earlier that when the micro is told to INPUT something, it displays a prompt (?), waits for a keyboard entry + (R), assigns what was entered to a variable, and then goes on. When we first met INPUT, it concerned the keyboard entry of a number. Now it concerns the keyboard entry of a string—anything that's not a number.

A string is any set of keyboard characters All the messages we've used are strings; so too were the answers to questions like "And your house and street?". Strings can contain numbers, as your street address probably does, but they are *not* numbers—even if they contain nothing but numbers. If that's complicated—don't worry; I'll come back to it in detail later.

So PRINT can be used to display a string in one of two ways. In the case of PRINT "your message", the string "your message" is a *string constant* (an unchanging string). In the case of PRINT NAME$, NAME$ is a string variable whose value must have been assigned to it before. So we can have:

1Ø	PRINT "What is your name";	[print string constant]
2Ø	INPUT X$	[assign to string variable]
3Ø	PRINT X$	[print string variable]

or even

1Ø	Y$ = "Watch Panorama!"	[assign constant to string variable]
2Ø	PRINT Y$	[print it]

Try the next program, and see some of these points in practice.

Program 5: Favourite colour

```
 1Ø   MODE 5
 2Ø   COLOUR 129
 3Ø   COLOUR 3
 4Ø   MYCOLOUR$ = "RED"              [change this if you want!]
 5Ø   MESSAGE$ = "What colour do you like best?"
 6Ø   REPEAT
 7Ø   CLS
 8Ø   PRINT ' ' TAB (1); MESSAGE$;
 9Ø   INPUT ANSWER$
1ØØ   UNTIL ANSWER$ = MYCOLOUR$
11Ø   PRINT ' ' MYCOLOUR$; "is my favourite too." ' ' '
      " Glad we agree!" ' ' ' ' ' '
```

ANIMATION WITH PRINT

First I want to extend the TAB idea a bit. We've seen how you can PRINT TAB (number) to reach any point on any line. Thus in MODE 5, PRINT TAB (122); "A" would put A in the position shown; while PRINT TAB (222); "B" would put B in a position 222 spaces from the start (see Figure 5.1). However to put a character in any position this way is both clumsy and hard to use. Also its result would depend on what else had already been printed. (Try PRINT TAB (122); "A"; TAB (222); "B", for instance.) Fortunately we can also use TAB (X, Y) to print directly at position X on line Y. Thus PRINT TAB (2, 22); "C" would give the result for C shown below.

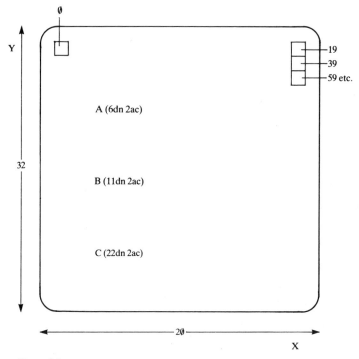

Figure 5.1

Try this little program out carefully.

```
10  MODE 5
20  COLOUR 128
30  COLOUR 3
40  CLS
50  PRINT ' ' "Line";
60  INPUT ROW
70  PRINT ' ' "Column";
80  INPUT COLUMN
90  PRINT ' ' "Character";
```

```
100   INPUT CHARACTER$
110   PRINT TAB (COLUMN, ROW); CHARACTER$
```

If you *did* try this carefully, you should have noticed some strange things. Thus strange effects follow PRINT TABing outside the screen limits: MODE 5 has 32 lines of twenty spaces. But the most important thing to note is that the first line is number Ø and the first column is number Ø. PRINT TAB (Ø, Ø) puts you at the top left corner of the screen. And you can't stick at the bottom right corner—position (19, 31)—because the prompt messes things up. (We'll get over that later.)

Anyway, let's animate. Here's a game (of sorts). Enter it, try it—and try to see what I'm doing. I'll put comments in where really necessary of course.

Program 6: Flit

```
 10   MODE 5
 20   COLOUR 128
 30   COLOUR Ø
 40   CLS
 50   X = 9
 60   Y = 14
 70   FLIT = Ø
 80   REPEAT
 90   VDU 7                           [beep from speaker]
100   FLIT = FLIT + 1                 [count flits]
110   PRINT TAB (X − 1, Y − 1); "□ □ □"; TAB (X − 1, Y);
      "□ * □"; TAB (X − 1, Y + 1); "□ □ □"
120   A = RND (2)
130   IF A = 1   X = X − 1
140   IF A = 2   X = X + 1
150   A = RND (2)
160   IF A = 1   Y = Y − 1
170   IF A = 2   Y = Y + 1
180   FOR A = 1 TO 55Ø: NEXT         [a delay loop]
190   UNTIL X = Ø OR X = 19 OR Y = Ø OR Y = 31
200   PRINT TAB (Ø, 9); "Fly lasted"; FLIT; "flits"
```

Don't worry about the "delay loop" in line 18Ø—it slows the "fly" down, but how it works, I'll come back to later.

However, everything else should be clear if you think a bit. And the whole idea's very important. This program is an exercise in TAB, so be particularly sure you understand lines 12Ø–17Ø and 11Ø.

YOUR OWN CHARACTERS

Actually the BBC asterisk (*) that I used in the last program makes quite a nice fly. But this micro allows you to make up your own characters if you want.

A tiny bit of theory first. Computers like the Beeb can have up to 256 different characters in their *character set*. These have numbers from Ø to 255.

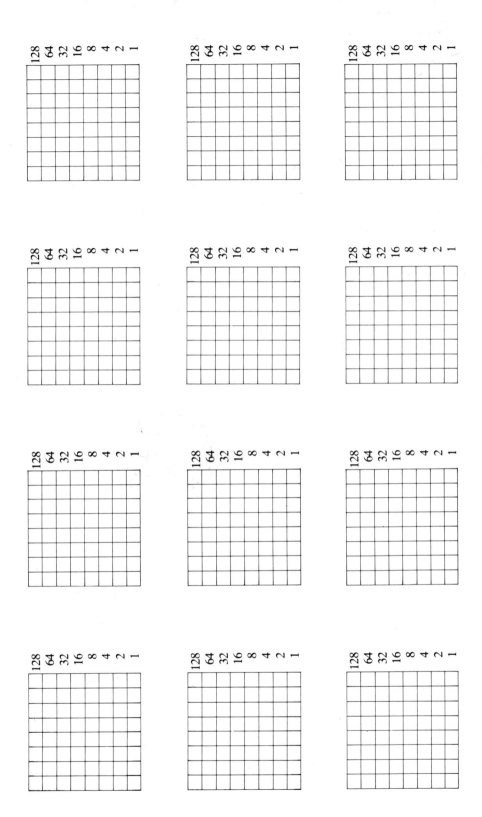

Figure 5.2

256 characters is a lot. Add up what you can think of:

Upper-case letters	26
Lower-case letters	26
Digits	1∅
Punctuation signs	11
Mathematical ones	9
Other symbols (£ etc.)	3 or so
Space	1

A lot less than a hundred! Some computers offer lots of special shapes (graphics blocks), like card symbols and shapes for building pictures. Others put the keywords (IF, PRINT, TAB, INPUT and so on) in as single characters. The BBC micro gives you the facility of designing your own characters and storing them in memory for use where required. If you have designed character 224 to be the Greek alpha (α), then you can get it when you want by PRINT CHR$ (224)—print the character whose number is 224. To define your shapes is a bit lengthy. Be warned! But it's worth it.

1. You need to sketch your shape on an 8 × 8 grid. Use old graph paper or pages from a square ruled exercise book, or make copies of the grids in Figure 5.2.
2. Sketch your design faintly on the 8 × 8 grid. A sketch for alpha is shown in Figure 5.3.
3. Reproduce the shape as close to that sketch as you can by blacking in the right squares of the grid, Figure 5.4.

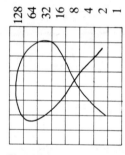

Figure 5.3

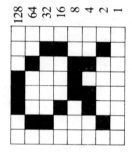

Figure 5.4

4. Now—the tricky bit. Refer to Figure 5.5 to make it easier . . . For each of the eight lines of eight squares in turn—write down the sum of the numbers at the tops of the columns containing blacked-in squares. First line—no black squares, gives ∅; second line—black for squares 32 + 16 + 2, gives 5∅; and so on. CHECK MY ARITHMETIC!
5. Enter 1 VDU 23, 224, ∅, 5∅, 76, 136, 14∅, 148, 98, ∅. Here we are defining, with VDU 23, the character number 224 to be coded with those eight numbers.

∅	∅
32 + 16 + 2	5∅
64 + 8 + 4	76
128 + 8	136
128 + 8 + 4	14∅
128 + 16 + 4	148
64 + 32 + 2	98
∅	∅

Figure 5.5

Here's the rest of the program to test that first line.

```
10  MODE 5
20  COLOUR 129
30  COLOUR 2
40  CLS
50  PRINT TAB (10, 10); CHR$ (224)
```

OK—see what's happened? We've got an alpha on screen at position (10, 10). If you look at it closely you can just about see it's made up of dots like those I sketched.

Now the graphic design world is your oyster! Try your own shapes, giving them character numbers between 224 and 255 inclusive. (You can use others, but they will replace existing shapes.)

The sketch, Figure 5.6, and the program beside it, could give us a better fly for Program 6.

```
1   VDU 23, 225, 130, 198, 170, 170, 124,
    84, 124, 84

10  MODE 5

20  COLOUR 129

30  COLOUR 0

40  CLS

50  [etc. as before (with print CHR$ (225)
    instead of "*" in line 110) ]
```

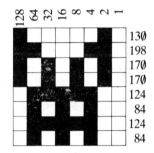

Figure 5.6

And here's a couple more you can try if you want:

```
VDU  23, 226, 32, 112, 82, 60, 60, 36, 108, 0
VDU  23, 227, 36, 90, 165, 90, 60, 155, 24, 60
```

Try your own Space Invader shape. I bet a few thousand other people already have! You can make bigger designs, if you like, by (literally) stringing shapes together. Here's the front half of a pantomime horse:

```
VDU  23, 225, 96, 172, 255, 223, 31, 40, 68, 130
```

Here's the back half:

```
VDU  23, 227, 0, 14, 250, 250, 248, 40, 68, 130
```

And here's the whole thing:

```
X$ = CHR$ (225) + CHR$ (227)
```

PRINT X$ in any mode (except 7) and see that lovely horse. Well, I'm no artist.

It's worth noting, by the way, that once a character is programmed like this, it stays in computer memory until it's re-programmed or you switch off.

SUMMARY

PRINT followed by nothing—skip a line
PRINT followed by something—start printing on next line
PRINT ' something—start on next line but one
PRINT; something—leave no space
PRINT, something—print in zone
PRINT TAB (n); something—leave n spaces then print
PRINT TAB (m, n); something—start printing at line n, column m

25

And the somethings?

> PRINT numeric constant; e.g. PRINT 4 gives 4
> PRINT numeric variable; e.g. PRINT A gives 4 if A has the value 4
> PRINT string constant; e.g. PRINT "A" gives A
> PRINT string variable; e.g. PRINT A$ gives * if A$ has the value *
> PRINT CHR$ (n) prints the character whose code is n

A versatile instruction indeed!

Now—it's up to you. We've looked at animation with PRINT, and you've got the hang of programming your own characters, so, what can you do now?

If you're short of ideas, try some of the projects. Or you should be able to follow most of Program A2, Train-race, at the back of the book. Enjoy yourself!

PROJECTS

1. Prepare a grid of small squares (using graph paper is a good idea), 20 across and 32 down. Plot on it a chart of the stars of your Zodiac sign. Write a program in MODE 5 with black background and yellow foreground to print out the starfield. Use * for each star, of course, and TAB (x, y) and TAB (x) for print positions.
2. With the same approach, write a program to display a picture of your choice. Study the keyboard characters, and experiment with them, to find which are most useful for "graphics blocks".
3. Enter, run and study Program 7. Make sure you understand (a) how it handles strings, (b) how it TABs, and (c) how I've involved VDU 23.

Program 7: Favourite food

```
 10   MODE 5
 20   COLOUR 130
 30   COLOUR 1
 40   VDU 23, 224, 170, 85, 170,
      85, 170, 85, 170, 85            [a useful character this!]
 50   A$ = "CARROTS"
 60   B$ = "BAKED BEANS"
 70   C$ = "TOMATO"
 80   D$ = "TOMATO KETCHUP"
 90   X$ = CHR$ (224)                  [shorter form]
100   CLS
110   PRINT TAB (20); "Your
      favourite food? [19 equals signs]"   [underline technique]
120   PRINT TAB (2, 10); "1.□"; A$     ⎤
130   PRINT TAB (22); "2.□"; B$        ⎟
140   PRINT ' TAB (2); "3.□"; C$;      ⎬— "menu"
150   PRINT TAB (42); "4.□"; D$        ⎦
160   PRINT ''''''
170   FOR A = 1 TO 2000: NEXT A        [delay]
180   PRINT "Please enter number, and RETURN." ''
190   INPUT A
200   IF A < 1 OR A > 4 THEN GOTO 190  [a simple error-trap]
```

```
210   CLS
220   PRINT TAB (1, 15); "Here you are then!"
230   FOR B = 1 TO 4000: NEXT B          [delay]
240   CLS
250   GOTO (200 + A * 100)               [useful trick—check it!]
300   PRINT TAB (5, 5); X$ ' TAB (4); X$;
      X$; X$' TAB (4); X$; X$;
      X$ ' TAB (4); X$; X$:
      X$ ' TAB (5); X$                   [there are easier ways!]
310   PRINT TAB (15, 15); X$ ' TAB (14);
      X$; X$; X$ ' TAB (14); X$; X$;
      X$ ' TAB (14); X$; X$;
      X$ ' TAB (15); X$
320   PRINT TAB (2, 20); A$
330   FOR B = 1 TO 4000: NEXT B
340   GOTO 100                           [re-start]
400   A = 1
410   REPEAT
420   PRINT TAB (RND (19),
      RND (31) ); X$
430   A = A + 1
440   UNTIL A = 50
450   PRINT TAB (2); B$
460   FOR B = 1 TO 4000: NEXT B
470   GOTO 100
500   PRINT ' ' ' ' ' ' TAB (9); X$
510   PRINT TAB (8); X$; X$; X$
520   PRINT TAB (7); X$; X$; X$; X$; X$ ' TAB (8);
      X$; X$; X$; TAB (9); X$
530   PRINT ' ' C$
540   FOR B = 1 TO 4000 ; NEXT B
550   GOTO 100
600   PRINT ' ' ' ' '
610   PRINT TAB (12); X$ ' TAB (11); X$; X$; X$;
      TAB (11); X$; X$; X$; TAB (11); X$; X$; X$;
      TAB (11); X$; X$; X$; TAB (11); X$; X$; X$
620   PRINT TAB (202); D$
630   FOR B = 1 TO 4000; NEXT B
640   GOTO 100
```

in some books, this counts as a whole program; they call it MEASLES

Note To get out of this, use ESCAPE (or BREAK).

4. Now practise your character-defining technique!
   (a) Re-write the program of project 1, defining five different sized dots or blobs for stars of different brightnesses.
   (b) Define your own graphics blocks, to make better pictures as in project 2.
   (c) Do the same to get more life-like food in Program 7.

6 Mind Your Language

As we've seen, everything a computer does is the result of instructions given to it by someone. All instructions must be in a form that the computer can act on. The instructions must be in the correct code, or language, if the micro is to understand.

Often the most efficient way of instructing a computer is to use a "low-level language", such as its specific "machine code" or "assembler". Efficient that may be, but easy it is not. In this book we shall not go as far as low-level programming—it is very interesting, and very rewarding, but best left to another time!

BBC AND OTHER BASICS

Until only a couple of decades ago, programmers had to work in low-level language. But then the concept of the high-level language was developed; BBC BASIC is a high-level language.

Instructions given in a high level-language often look much like "real" English. This means that they are easy for the programmer, but on the other hand, the computer must turn them into machine code before it can do anything with them. This translation takes time and memory so is not highly efficient.

There are hundreds of high-level languages. I am sure you have heard of some, like COBOL and FORTRAN. Apart from the BASIC we get with the BBC, a few other high-level languages are likely to appear for use with this micro in due course. (That will need different chips.)

The aims of each high-level language include ease of use, versatility and independence. That last means that a program in the given language will be acceptable to any machine running the language. Unfortunately this is rarely the case.

BASIC, in particular, because it is offered by more types of computer than any other language, suffers badly from the problem that each machine's version (dialect) is different from the rest.

BBC BASIC is more advanced than a number of other versions, and that is good. But it does mean that BBC BASIC programs need some changes before other computers can run them, and vice versa.

As you are likely to want to try programs written for other computers on your BBC machine, here are some notes to help you. However, these notes cannot claim to be anything like comprehensive. Always refer to the *Manual* for detail.

COMPLETELY DIFFERENT

There is little, if any, relationship between the ways one can program certain things on different micros. The BBC's MODE, COLOUR, SOUND and graphics (drawing) facilities are unique to it. Some computers don't offer those features at all. Those that do tend to use different keywords and different statement structures. Be careful of differences in numbers of characters in a line. Use the programmable character system

(VDU 23, page 24) where a program calls for special keyboard symbols (as do the Sinclairs and PETs, for instance).

The use of machine code/assembler routines in BASIC programs is fairly common. Keywords to watch out for are PEEK and POKE (BBC uses "?"), USR and CALL—but what one peeks or pokes or accesses by USR or CALL will differ greatly from machine to machine.

OTHER DIFFERENCES

TAB The BBC TAB (m, n) replaces the AT of some other machines—but check the details of the numbers that follow it.

LET Some computers expect LET in assignment statements: LET X = 4 rather than the BBC's X = 4. The BBC does, however, understand LET if you use it to make assignments clearer.

GOTO Some programmers use GOTO a lot, though BBC BASIC doesn't much need it. As a program statement GOTO 150 means skip over to line 150 and go on from there. As a command, GOTO 300 means start running the program from line 300. If you use this useful trick, remember that the line must exist—some computers, if told to go to a line that doesn't exist will start at the next higher line they find. With the BBC computer you cannot use RUN followed by a line number.

END Some computers must have END as the last line of a BASIC program. This is not needed with the BBC machine—but, as with LET, it accepts it.

Variable names Although of any length you like, in BBC BASIC the variable names can contain only letters, numbers and dashes (the dash is below the £); the first must be a letter. The names of files (which is what we call programs and data saved on tape) are a bit less restricted. These can be any combination of up to ten characters, except that the first cannot be a space. Do not use keywords inside variable names (TO, LET, etc.).

Functions (which we'll look at in a bit more detail later) are things like SIN and LOG, that you may have met in school maths. These need brackets in many BASICs. You can use brackets with the BBC, but don't have to, except to make the meaning clear. Thus you can have PRINT SIN (30) or PRINT SIN 30.

Spaces are required in BBC statements only if the meaning is not otherwise clear. So we can have PRINTSIN30 or PRINT SIN30 or PRINTSIN 30 or PRINT SIN 30—the computer will accept all these, so you may use whichever suits you. Some computer BASICs are very strict about where spaces must appear. Others put in spaces for you, but not necessarily where *you* want them. Of course the BBC micro will not accept extra spaces as in PR INTSIN30—again this is like most micros, except those that have keywords entered with a single key-stroke.

Power (exponentiation)—2 × 2 × 2 (two times two times two) may also be thought of as 2^3 (two to the power three, or two cubed). The BBC structure for raising a number to a power uses the symbol ↑ (on the key below BREAK)—PRINT 2 ↑ 3. Some computers use **. (Note that the symbol for divide is / (bottom row), as in PRINT 12/4, giving 3. The BBC micro is unusual in having the symbol ÷ in some modes; it uses the tilde, ~, on the ↑ key.)

Note: There are other differences between BBC BASIC and the dialects of other machines. However, what I've jotted down above covers the most important things, and will give you a good start to converting published programs into BBC BASIC.

7 A Colourful Computer

Getting colour into your BBC programs is a complex affair. You may know that some other computers have colour keys—just pressing the key gives you the colour you want. The BBC micro is not programmed like that, but does offer you a much more flexible colour control system—once you have got used to it!

The program fragment that follows is like the way we have started many programs off already. Let's start from scratch.

1. BREAK (and NEW if you haven't just switched on).
2. *KEY Ø "RUN ¦ M"—red key fØ gives RUN.
    *KEY 1Ø "OLD ¦ M LIST ¦ M"—BREAK key gives BREAK + LIST.
3. The fragment—after you enter each line, use fØ to check the effect and BREAK to get back to the list.

    1Ø   MODE 5

    2Ø   COLOUR 129

    3Ø   COLOUR 2

    4Ø   CLS

And now some points. The effects of the colour commands depend on the MODE you are in. So if line 1Ø were not there, 2Ø and 3Ø would have no effect. Also lines 2Ø and 3Ø do not show their effect until we do something else, such as instruct the screen to clear (line 4Ø, CLS).

So what does COLOUR do? Well, what it does is define the colours used when printing text. The background colour is given by a number greater than 127; the text colour itself depends on a number less than that. Table 7.1 shows the numbers and colours we can get in MODE 5 using COLOUR.

Table 7.1

Colour	Background	Text (foreground)
Black	COLOUR 128†	COLOUR Ø
Red	COLOUR 129	COLOUR 1
Yellow	COLOUR 13Ø	COLOUR 2
White	COLOUR 131	COLOUR 3†

The two values marked † are called "default" values. They are what you get automatically in MODE 5 (and all the others) unless you instruct the computer to do something else. So if you *want* white text on a black background, you don't need to use COLOUR at all. That seems logical!

I'm going to take a break from colour for a minute, to tell you about FOR . . . NEXT loops. That's because I want to use them in colour demonstration routines. Put your four lines on to key f1 for later use:

*KEY 1 "MODE 5 ¦ M COLOUR 129 ¦ M COLOUR 2 ¦ M CLS ¦ M"

FOR . . . NEXT LOOPS

As we saw when we met REPEAT (page 12), a loop is a set of program lines that the micro cycles through a number of times. We use REPEAT . . . UNTIL for a loop when we don't know how many times to go round. (I also often use it as the last line in a program, to prevent the prompt re-appearing and to disable the keyboard—like this 999 REPEAT: UNTIL FALSE.)

When we *do* know how many times to loop we can use the FOR . . . NEXT structure. I used it once already, to set up a certain delay, before the computer went on to something else. Here is *that* structure:

FOR Z = 1 TO 1000: NEXT Z

This gives a delay of about a second, during which the computer goes round the (empty) loop a thousand times. In a second! Here's a FOR . . . NEXT loop that's a bit more meaningful. Enter it (after BREAK/NEW), so we can explore it.

70   FOR NUMBER = 1 TO 100

80   PRINT; NUMBER; "☐";

90   NEXT NUMBER

RUN with f0 and try to explain what is happening; Figure 7.1 should help. What "FOR A = B TO C NEXT A" does is:

1.   Set up the variable A, giving it the starting value B (already defined).
2.   Carry out the statements inside the loop.
3.   On finding NEXT A, return to the start of the loop and step the value of A up by one. (Note that with the BBC, NEXT without the variable is accepted.)
4.   Keep doing this until A has reached the value C, when the program leaves the loop.

Modify the above little program like this and try it out a few times:

10   PRINT "First";

20   INPUT FIRST

30   PRINT "Last";

40   INPUT LAST

70   FOR NUMBER =. FIRST TO LAST

80   PRINT; NUMBER; "☐";

90   NEXT NUMBER

100   PRINT NUMBER

Are you happy with how it works? (Refer again to Figure 7.1 if necessary.) You should at least notice that the real last value of NUMBER is greater than you might think. (Line 100 shows this.) That means you must take care if you use the loop variable again after the loop is finished. But I hope you found other problems. Did you try decimal numbers, zero, negative numbers among your inputs? Did you try a value of LAST below the value of FIRST?

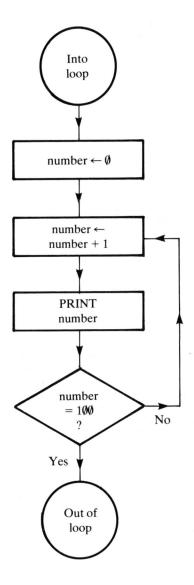

Figure 7.1

33

Most BASICs, including the BBC dialect, extend FOR . . . TO . . . NEXT with the possibility of different step sizes. That is, the loop variable (NUMBER in our example) can go up by jumps other than 1. Modify the program again to show this; it is now the final version, so why not sketch an up-dated diagram of it too?

Program 8: The FOR . . . NEXT loop

```
 10   PRINT "First";
 20   INPUT FIRST
 30   PRINT "Last";
 40   INPUT LAST
 50   PRINT "Step";
 60   INPUT S                          [S not STEP—why?]
 70   CLS
 80   PRINT TAB (4); "Number"; TAB (16); "Cube"
 90   PRINT TAB (4); "= = = = = ="; TAB (16); "= = = ="
100   FOR NUMBER = FIRST TO LAST STEP S
110   PRINT NUMBER, NUMBER ↑ 3        [see page 42]
120   NEXT NUMBER
```

Play around with that as you will. (You will find a BBC BASIC arithmetic problem, no doubt—but we'll deal with that later.) But I wanted to do FOR . . . NEXT loops now so we could investigate colour a bit more deeply. Remember?

CHANGING COLOUR

Use BREAK/NEW to clear out the FOR program. We still have our colour introduction on key f1. Here's how to get it into our next program. The technique uses the nice AUTO facility. We met it before—it automatically feeds you line numbers from 10 up in steps of 10 (unless you tell it otherwise, and until you ESCAPE).

So—enter AUTO (R), and 10 appears. Now press f1, and there are the first four lines of our colour program! ESCAPE to allow you to use your own line numbers and enter this "procedure"—COLOURTEST. (Yes, I'll come back to procedures more fully later.)

```
 999   REPEAT: UNTIL FALSE            [stops program]
1000   DEF PROCCOLOURTEST             [no space allowed after PROC]
1010   CLS
1020   FOR STAR = 1 TO 640
1030   PRINT "*";                     [note semi-colon]
1040   NEXT STAR
1050   FOR WAIT = 1 TO 1000    ⎤
1060   NEXT WAIT              ⎦— delay loop
1070   ENDPROC                        [no space allowed before PROC]
```

The above lines, apart from 999, define the procedure we've called COLOURTEST. (999 simply separates the procedures from the main program.) The value of a procedure is that we can call for it to be used whenever we want. Like this!

```
 50   PROCCOLOURTEST                  [no spaces allowed]
```

RUN (f 0) — to get a red screen full of yellow stars. The keyboard is disabled by line 999; use BREAK to get back to the listing. Now we can start colour changes! Add:

    60   COLOUR 128
    70   COLOUR 3
    80   PROCCOLOURTEST

OK? This shows we can use COLOUR when we like in a program, to change text and/or background colour.

The main program's a bit clumsy though—sure, you can change each colour statement in turn to investigate the effect. But let's try looping through all the possibilities . . . We're going to need new lines from 20 to 80; and a few other changes:

    20   FOR COLB = 128 TO 131   [COLB—background colour]
    30   FOR COLT = 0 TO 3   [COLT—text colour]
    40   IF COLB = 128 + COLT THEN
         GOTO 80   [Why?]
    50   COLOUR COLB
    60   COLOUR COLT
    70   PROCCOLOURTEST
    80   NEXT COLT
    90   NEXT COLB

and

    1033   PRINT TAB (0, 10); "Background □"; COLB ' "Text □"; COLT

Line 1033 tells the computer to display the names of the colours being used each time. If you want more time to read the message, increase the last value in the delay loop (line 1050).

That program shows how one can use the four different colours for text and background allowed in MODE 5. However, the BBC micro has on offer sixteen colours (or colour arrangements). In MODE 2 (Model B) one can access all of these on screen at once. However in MODE 5 one can select any four for MODE 5. This is done by using a VDU statement to re-define the colours normally allowed.

Look again at the list of "normal" colours in Table 7.1 (at the beginning of this chapter).

Having entered MODE 5, we use VDU 19 . . . to re-define any of those. Thus VDU 19, 128, 4; 0; (note the strange punctuation) will make background 128 blue instead of black. The colour options and their numbers are as follows.

Colour option	VDU 19 code	Flashing option	VDU 19 code
Black	0	Black/white	8
Red	1	Red/cyan	9
Green	2	Green/magenta	10
Yellow	3	Yellow/blue	11
Blue	4	Blue/yellow	12
Magenta	5	Magenta/green	13
Blue-green (cyan)	6	Cyan/red	14
White	7	White/black	15

Using VDU 19 gives a remarkable range of effects. It's tough going to get on top of this facility, but I'll now add to our existing colour program a routine to demonstrate it. Then it'll be up to you!

Program 9: Rainbow stars

10	MODE 5	[colour mode]
20	FOR COLB = 128 TO 131	[background colours]
30	FOR COLT = 0 TO 3	[text colours]
40	IF COLB = COLT THEN GOTO 80	[skip "invisible" combinations]
50	COLOUR COLB	
60	COLOUR COLT	
70	PROCCOLOURTEST	
80	NEXT COLT	
90	NEXT COLB	
100	COLOUR 128	[start afresh]
110	COLOUR 1	
120	FOR COLB = 1 TO 15	
130	FOR COLT = 1 TO 15	
140	PROCCOLOURTEST	
150	VDU 19, 1, COLT; 0;	[re-define text colour]
160	NEXT COLT	
170	VDU 19, 128, COLB; 0;	[re-define background colour]
180	NEXT COLB	
999	−1070	[DEFine PROCedure COLOURTEST as before]

As I say, it's up to you whether to go further or not at this stage. I shall have to take another look at colour programming when we get to BBC graphics, so you can skip it now if you want. Here, meanwhile, some projects on what we've done so far.

PROJECTS

1. Write a MODE 5 program to flash the screen red-yellow-red a hundred times. If it doesn't work first time (and I bet it doesn't), try slowing it down!
2. Re-write Program 2 or 4 and Program 5 using FOR . . . NEXT instead of REPEAT . . . UNTIL. Try to understand the situations in which each loop structure is the better.
3. Experiment with:
   (a) changing colour in mid-screen;
   (b) the flashing facility.
   (Experimentation is the best way to get on top of VDU 19!)
4. Write a program offering the user choice of colour from the main six, giving him/her a screen of that colour, and then . . . I don't know, *you* think of something.

36

8 Improving Your Command

In this chapter I'd like to draw your attention to rather a ragbag of BBC facilities that will make your programming faster and more effective. First, let me use the opportunity to remind you of the main commands we've met. (A command is an instruction for the computer that's entered directly, without a line number, and carried out at once.)

COMMANDS

We have so far met four commands of use when there's a program in memory. These are OLD, LIST, RUN and NEW. Each needs to be typed out and followed by the return (R) key before being carried out (executed).

OLD must be used after BREAK to allow you to access again the program in memory. If you use BREAK and enter a number, followed by any character and (R), the computer "assumes" that you've put in a line number of a new program. It then clears the old lines from its memory. Always use OLD after BREAK then, if you want to keep that program.

LIST displays on screen, in line-number order, the current program instructions. This command has several forms.

> LIST displays the whole program.
> LIST n displays only line number n (if it exists).
> LIST n, shows the whole program from line n onwards.
> LIST, n shows the whole program up to line n.
> LIST n, m displays the section from line n to line m.

When you have a program of more than a couple of dozen lines LIST by itself becomes rather cumbersome. It's not easy to find the bit you need to look at, nor is it easy to edit. (I'm coming to edit in a minute.)

If the program has more than 24 lines it can't all fit on to the screen at once. The list then "scrolls" through until the last line is displayed. LIST such and such gets over that. You may prefer instead to stop the scrolling action. That is done by entering "CTRL N". CTRL is the CONTROL key (marked CTRL, over on the left of the keyboard); to use it, hold it down while pressing the N key. The BBC will no longer scroll, until you get back by using CTRL O or BREAK—CTRL N has put you in "page mode". In page mode press the SHIFT key to move on.

Another LIST range is called "list option", the keyword being LISTO (*not* LISTØ). Using this will get the BBC to force spaces into your listings, to make them more readable (but take up more memory). The number you use with LISTO fixes exactly how this is done. The options are shown overleaf.

LISTO 0 no spaces (= LIST)	LISTO 4 indentation in REPEAT loops
LISTO 1 spaces after line-numbers	LISTO 5 = LISTO 1 + LISTO 4
LISTO 2 indentation in FOR loops	LISTO 6 = LISTO 2 + LISTO 4
LISTO 3 = LISTO 1 + LISTO 2	LISTO 7 = LISTO 1 + LISTO 2 + LISTO 4

After LISTO n, whenever you list, you'll get your option of spaces. So if you want all possible spaces and indentations, enter LISTO 7 (R). Whenever you LIST thereafter, you will find the posh program layout that some books and magazines use for maximum clarity. (There is a problem with LISTO, though; when you're editing you'll find it can force in extra spaces on edited lines that can make the result very untidy. Because of this I don't use LISTO until I've given my program its final polish.)

RUN should present no problems by now. It tells the computer to start executing the current program from the first line. It also sets all the variable values to zero; if that is not what you want, use GOTO n (first line-number) instead. The command GOTO such and such is also useful in other cases:

1. When you want to start execution from inside a program, to test how one part works, for instance.
2. When you have several separate programs in memory, and want to execute any but the first. The sketch should make this clearer (Figure 8.1).

Some micros let you use RUN n in such cases; the BBC machine does not.

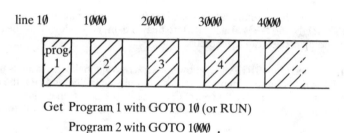

line 10   1000   2000   3000   4000

Get Program 1 with GOTO 10 (or RUN)

Program 2 with GOTO 1000 .

etc.

Figure 8.1

NEW finally, is not new either (ho, ho). Use it to remove the current program from memory and put all variable values to zero. NEW does not de-program the red function keys or the CONTROL instructions you've previously entered. Some folk don't bother with NEW, but avoid their mistake! If the new program doesn't use exactly the same line-numbers as the old one, you're going to get a craxy mixed-up program—a combo of instructions from two programs in one. I guess that won't work the way you want!

EDITING

By now you'll be needing to know about editing, so read through this bit, perhaps practising on a program in memory—and get used to the techniques.

The full set of editing facilities—ways to change program lines—on the Beeb is fairly versatile. That makes it a bit cumbersome if you're not careful.

The simplest form of editing concerns the complete removal of one or more lines of a program. That's easy! You just enter the line-number in question followed by (R). The line has now nothing in it, so is nothing—and it vanishes from the LIST. But *do* be sure you want to remove the line before doing this!

The same kind of technique allows you to replace an existing line with a new version. Thus if line 50 is PRINT A$ and you want it to be INPUT A$, just enter 50 INPUT A$ (R)—and this is now in the list insead of the old form.

Fine so far—but it's a bit of a drag to go through all that if the old and new lines are lengthy, or if minor changes are needed to many lines. Then we can call on the Beeb's *full* range of editing facilities. These use the four *cursor control* keys—the set of four on the right with arrows in different directions on them—plus the COPY key at the bottom right corner of the keyboard.

Press the COPY key now. It will beep at you, sadly pointing out that there is nothing for it to copy. So let's give it something to copy. Enter a couple of fairly complex program lines. Something like these:

    10   PRINT "This line is wrong."

    20   PRINT "This line needs copying."

How can we correct line 10 to make it right? We may want it to read 10 PRINT "Now this line is right." We could do it by just entering the new version, but let's try screen editing. Press the up-cursor key twice. The dash prompt moves up screen to lie next to the 1 of line 10. (The other prompt stays where it was.) Press the COPY key for about a second. No beep now—the result is that the first few characters of line 10 appear—are copied—beside the prompt. Follow through this sequence of key-presses; I'm starting again.

Action	Result by > prompt	Effect on _ prompt
1. ↑↑	None	Up two lines
2. COPYYYYYYYYYY (repeated)	> 10 PRINT	Across ten places: _"
3. Apostrophe	> 10 PRINT '	None
4. COPYY	> 10 PRINT ' "T	Across two places: h
5. DELETE	> 10 PRINT ' "	None
6. Now t	> 10 PRINT ' "Now t	None
7. COPYYYYYYYYYYYY	> 10 PRINT ' "Now this line is_	Across twelve places: w
8. right."	> 10 PRINT ' "Now this line is right."	
(R)	> _	Returns next to >

Complicated? Well, maybe. Easier to do than describe. Let me summarize. The cursor control keys can move the _ cursor anywhere on the screen. When you press COPY, by the > prompt appears the characters underlined by the _ cursor. This goes on until you stop pressing COPY. At any stage you can delete one or more characters (with the DELETE key) or insert one or more by typing them as usual. When you press RETURN, the end of the line is assumed and we return to the usual position.

Try to use these keys—cursor control, COPY, DELETE and RETURN—to get the following versions of line 10.

    10   PRINT "This line is very wrong, this line is."

    10   PRINT "This line is wrong, wrong, wrong."

We can edit line-numbers as well, to give new ones. Work out how to use edit to repeat line 20 in lines 30, 40 and 50. Finally, edit line 10, to read:

    10   PRINT ' "This line is wrong, wrong, wrong—it needs copying."

When you edit in practice, take note of this final tip. Use LIST n, m to get just the few lines you want to work with. Otherwise the process takes a lot longer and is more open to mistakes.

Mistakes? Well, there is one very easy trap to fall into. While editing a line, do *not* press RETURN after insertions/deletions, but COPY the rest of the line first. Otherwise you'll end up with only half the line you want.

SQUASHING PROGRAMS

The BBC offers two facilities for reducing programming time and memory. The first is that keywords can be abbreviated; the second is that more than one statement can be placed on a single line. The first saves programming time and reduces typing errors; the second reduces memory and can make listings easier to follow.

Abbreviated keywords are acceptable to the micro when you are entering commands or instructions. There is a complete list in the *User Guide*. In each case, enter one or two letters plus a full stop instead of the full word. Thus you can use P. for PRINT, L. for LIST and AU. for AUTO. When the abbreviated instructions are listed, they appear in the usual full form.

This is obviously a useful technique for common keywords. However it's not worth the trouble of thinking about it in less common cases. Thinking *is* necessary, as, with well over a hundred keywords, the abbreviation used cannot be just the first letter.

Here is a list of the keywords met so far, and the abbreviated form.

AUTO	AU.	MODE	MO.
CHAIN	CH.	NEW	NEW†
CHR$	CHR.†	NEXT	N.
CLS	CLS†	OLD	O.
COLOUR	C.	PRINT	P.
END	END†	PROC	PRO.†
ENDPROC	E.	REPEAT	REP.
FALSE	FA.	RND	RND†
FOR	F.	RUN	RUN†
GCOL	GC.	STEP	S.
GOTO	G.	TAB	TAB†
IF	IF†	THEN	TH.
INPUT	I.	TO	TO†
LET	LET†	UNTIL	U.
LIST	L.		

Those marked † are either not abbreviations or not worth using. You may think the latter about some of the others too!

To confuse the matter further (but to be complete) note also that you can use longer abbreviations than those shown if you want—IN. or INP. (or even INPU.) for INPUT is an example. In future, when I introduce new keywords, if I tell you the abbreviated form you can use that if you want.

Multiple statements on a line is the posh term for structures like the following; we've already used this one in fact:

   100   FOR WAIT = 1 TO 1000: NEXT WAIT

This contains two statements (FOR . . ., and NEXT . . .). There's nothing wrong with putting them on two lines, but they *can* go on one, with a colon (:) to show the boundary between them.

It is logical to use this technique in cases where a small number of lines have one specific task, as with the delay loop above. Do *not* overdo the approach, as it can make a program less easy to read. However you can have up to about twenty statements in one line if you wish. Here are more examples:

   120   REPEAT: STAR = STAR + 1: PRINT "*";: UNTIL STAR = 500

   130   CLS: PRINT TAB (0, 10); "Message";: INPUT ANSWER: CLS

The need to put PRINT "Message" close to INPUT such and such is so common that the BBC micro has a special squashing trick for that. Here it is

   150   INPUT "Message", ANSWER   [gives ? prompt]

or alternatively

    15Ø   INPUT "Message" ANSWER   [no prompt]

Here's the structure:

    line-number + INPUT "Message in quotes" + (,) + variable name.

The assigned variable can be a string or a number, of course. More than one input at a time can be accepted too. In other words, with the BBC you can use structures like this:

    2ØØ   P. "Enter three numbers, with RETURN after each";

    21Ø   I. N1, N2, N3

Both are in effect useful multiple statements-on-a-line techniques. Try them in *your* programs; note them in mine.

ODDMENTS

I want to note here a few other techniques met already but perhaps not fully explained.

The function keys Each of the red function keys and BREAK (key f1Ø in effect) can be programmed like this.

    *KEY 3 "FOR WAIT = 1 TO 1ØØ ¦ M NEXT WAIT ¦ M"

Here

    *KEY n is the command—program key number n . . .
    ". . ."—the instructions appear in a pair of quote marks
    ¦ M is the code for RETURN in this case.

As with multiple statements on a line, you can have one or more instructions between "and". You can, if you prefer, separate them with colons rather than with ¦ M—but you must close with ¦ M if you want to avoid using RETURN after using the programmed key. Note that you can use the *KEY instruction as part of a program if you want, though that hasn't many simple uses.

The DELETE key Each time you press this, the last character in the material being entered or edited is deleted. Keep the key down to delete a lot of characters. Users of your programs can use DELETE to correct an input answer before pressing RETURN. I wish I had a key like this on my typewriter; it's one of the nice things about text editing (word processing)—so easy to wipe out errors!

REPEAT If you hold any key down for more than about half a second, you will find its effect repeated as long as the key is down. This is particularly useful with cursor control, COPY and delete, but works on *all* keys. Underlining and printing patterns become very easy.

I've pushed every button I can find, but I still can't get the 9 o'clock News

9 Getting Your Sums Right

If you think about it for a moment, you'll realize that the word "computer" implies something for doing mathematical calculations. The first machines of this kind were certainly just programmable electronic calculators. (And they weren't as good at calculating, in many ways, as the calculators we can now buy for a few pounds.)

When I defined the computer near the beginning of this book, I spoke of it as a data processor. In fact whatever kind of data a computer processes, it all has to be represented in number form (binary numbers in fact) and all the processing consists of mathematical processes.

OK—that's not very relevant to us as users. But it *is* time to find out a bit more about arithmetic in BBC BASIC. We've met it quite a lot already, and I hope it didn't worry you. Anyway, let's look at this little program. Enter, use, consider.

Program 1∅: Four-function calculator

```
 10   MODE 5: COLOUR 13∅: COLOUR ∅        [arithmetic can be colourful!]
 2∅   REPEAT: CLS
 3∅   PRINT TAB (2∅); "Enter two numbers",
      "(RETURN after each)"
 4∅   INPUT NUM 1, NUM 2                   [note multiple INPUT]
 5∅   CLS: PRINT ' NUM 1, NUM 2
 6∅   PRINT ' ' "Sum", NUM 1 + NUM 2
 7∅   PRINT ' ' "Difference", NUM 1 − NUM 2
 8∅   PRINT ' ' "Product", NUM 1 * NUM 2
 9∅   PRINT ' ' "Quotient", NUM 1 / NUM 2
1∅∅   FOR WAIT = 1 TO 1∅∅∅: NEXT          [WAIT not needed at end]
11∅   PRINT TAB (∅, 25); "Press RETURN for",
      "next go."
12∅   INPUT N: UNTIL FALSE
```

Note the use of INPUT in line 12∅—it holds the display until the RETURN key is used. The input value, if any, is not used—this is simply a useful "hold" trick. Note, too, the double input at line 4∅. The message asks the user for two numbers separated by (R). In fact, you may note that it would also accept two numbers separated by a comma.

Anyway—the arithmetic. The above program shows simply how BBC BASIC (and all other BASICs) deals with the four main arithmetic functions: add, subtract, multiply and divide. Note (I've said it before) the special symbols * for "times" and / for divide.

We have also already met a fifth important function, given by ↑. The posh name for this is—wait for it—"exponentiation". I call it "raise to a power", but that's a mouthful too. Add this to the above program:

95   PRINT ' ' "Power", NUM 1 ↑ NUM 2

Again, try it.

I hope when you're running this program, you're testing it fully. What happens when you input decimal numbers, negative numbers, zero, and so on? What happens at line 90 if NUM 2 is zero? (Computers can't divide by zero—why not?) And—what would happen if we had more complex expressions to evaluate than those in Program 10? Think about this simple little problem . . .

Two children each have three ball-points and two felt-tips.
How many pens have they altogether?

OK, I know you can work it out in your head. But how do you do it? And, more important, how do you tell the computer to do it?

Does *this* give the right answer?—PRINT 2 * 3 + 2 (try it!). I hope you tried it; I hope you got the "wrong" answer. But computers can't make mistakes, can they? What's happened to the missing two pens?

Try *this* then—PRINT 3 + 2 * 2. After all, that's how you do it in your head, and it's how you would do it on a hand calculator. Wrong answer still! A *different* wrong answer.

So, there's a problem. It's not the computer's fault. The thing is that the machine is trained always to multiply before it adds. So it goes

$2 * 3 + 2 = 6 + 2 = 8$

and

$3 + 2 * 2 = 3 + 4 = 7$

The posh term for this is: multiply has a higher priority than add. If you want to break priority, as we do here, you have to use brackets: ( ). (Note that the BBC has square brackets too, but they're for something else, and don't work here.)

So, you must enter PRINT 2 * (3 + 2), and the computer goes $2 * (3 + 2) = 2 * 5 = 10$.

IF YOU DON'T PUT BRACKETS WHERE THEY'RE NEEDED, YOU'LL GET THE WRONG ANSWER . . . On the other hand, if you use them where they're *not* needed, you get the right answer. So—if in doubt, put them in.

Here is the BBC's priorities list:

Highest	(. . .)	brackets
	. . .	functions (like SIN)
↑	raise to power
	*, /	multiply, divide
Lowest	+, −	add, subtract

There are others in the full list, but we needn't worry about them here.

Now, if you're not mathematically minded, you're not likely to want to do much in the line of sophisticated number-crunching programming. You have my permission to skip the rest of this chapter, then—but please glance through the projects at the end. One day you'll come back . . .

NUMBER-CRUNCHING

Right—if you're still here, let's go on.

If you have a bit of a mathematical background, you may have come across things called quadratic equations. These are equations like $ax^2 + bx + c = 0$, where a, b, c are numbers (coefficients) and x is a variable. For any set of values of a, b and c, there can be no more than two values of x that fit the equation. These two values are the "roots" of x. We can find them like this:

$$\text{Root 1: } x_1 = \frac{-b + \sqrt{(b^2 - 4ac)}}{2a} \qquad \text{Root 2: } x_2 = \frac{-b - \sqrt{(b^2 - 4ac)}}{2a}$$

Here is a program to find the roots of x for any input set of a, b and c, if the roots exist. (They don't always!)

Program 11: Quadroots (improvements follow)

```
10   MODE 5: COLOUR 129: COLOUR 0: CLS
20   PRINT TAB (21); "Enter coefficients"
     ' TAB (1); "[18 equals signs]"              [underline]
30   INPUT ' ' ' " a = ", A
40   INPUT ' ' ' " b = ", B          ⎤  use EDIT to get
50   INPUT ' ' ' " c = ", C          ⎦  these from 30
60   X1 = (- B + SQR (B↑2 - 4 * A * C)) / 2 * A
70   X2 = (- B - SQR (B↑2 - 4 * A * C)) / 2 * A     [EDIT from 60]
80   PRINT ' ' ' " ROOTS: " ' ' X1 ' ' X2 ' '
90   FOR W = 1 TO 2000: NEXT:
     INPUT "Again", A: GOTO 10          [re-start]
```

The important lines to us here are 60 and 70. Study them in the light of what I have just said about priorities. And I *mean* study: for each line work out the order of computer operations and the need for each part.

SQR is the square root function. We can use it like this—P. SQR 4, giving 2—in simple cases; otherwise put brackets round the numerical expression as I did in Program 11.

The square root of a negative number has no real meaning and cannot be evaluated by the micro. Thus you will get the *error message* "−ve root at line 60" if a = b = c = 1. And the program stops. To avoid this kind of problem the BBC has a useful *error-trap* facility. The statement structure is ON ERROR . . .

Try this—it's worth bearing in mind, but needs *great* care in use:

```
65   ON ERROR PRINT ' "Not real" ' ' : GOTO 90
```

Now we've "trapped" the error—provided a more relevant message and avoided the program stopping.

The next function I'd like to discuss is called INT. Try the following direct commands to test what it does:

P. INT X where X is a set of numbers like 1.2, 1.25, 1.8, 0.1, 0 and similar negative ones.

I hope you can see that what INT X does is to return the whole number (integer) to the left of X on the number line. See the sketch, Figure 9.1. We can often use INT just like that. There are two particularly useful INT structures, though, that you should get to know. We'll use the second in a minute to make a further improvement to Program 11.

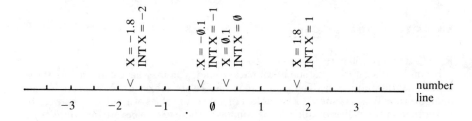

Figure 9.1

1. We can use INT to round a mixed number to the nearest whole number, to give 1 from 1.2, and 2 from 1.8 for instance. Here's the structure:

   X = INT (X + 0.5)

   Try it on a set of numbers as above; refer to the number line sketch if you can't see how it works.
2. We can also use INT to round a mixed number to a value correct to a given number of decimal places. To two decimal places, for instance (as when dealing with decimal money) we want 1.23 from anything between 1.225 and 1.234999 . . . Here's *this* structure:

   X = INT (X * 100 + 0.5) / 100

   Test it out fully as usual. Adapt it to give a different number of decimal places.

We can now go back to Program 11 and modify it to give roots correct to (say) four decimal places. Edit lines 60 and 70 to include INT like this:

   60   X1 = INT (((−B + SQR (B↑2 − 4 * A * C)) / 2 * A) * 10000 + 0.5) / 10000

OTHER FUNCTIONS

I'm just going to give you a bald list of the main mathematical functions offered by the Beeb, with short comments where necessary. If you're going to use any, I guess you'll have a fair idea of their meaning. Note the word "argument"—it's the official name of whatever the function acts on (don't ask me why).

ABS returns the absolute value of the argument. Thus ABS (4) = 4; ABS (−4) = 4. Its main simple use is to evaluate the absolute difference between two numbers:

   IF ABS (A − B) < 10 PRINT "Well done!" ELSE PRINT "Wrong!"

ACS, ASN, ATN return the values of the angles whose cosine, sine and tangent (respectively) are the arguments. The angles are given in radians:

   ASN 0.5 = 0.523 . . .

Use DEG to convert to degrees:

   DEG (ASN 0.5) = 30

COS, SIN, TAN give the cosine, sine and tangent (respectively) of the arguments. The arguments are assumed to be in radians:

   SIN 30 = −0.988 . . .

Use RAD to convert to radians:

   SIN (RAD 30) = 0.5

DEG converts radians to degrees (see ACS above).

DIV returns the whole number part of a division. (MOD gives the remainder.) The structure may look strange:

   P.100 DIV 9 gives 11 (whole number)
   P.100 MOD 9 gives 1 (remainder)
   P.100 DIV 9, 100 MOD 9 (both)

LOG gives the logarithm of the argument to base 10.

MOD See DIV above.

RAD See COS above.

RND We've looked at RND already. This gives some kind of (semi-) random number in a range depending on its argument, if any. For instance:

RND (12) could give 1, 2, 3, 4, 5, 6, 7, 8, 9, 1Ø, 11 or 12.

SGN is of occasional use. SGN X gives −1 if X is negative, Ø if X is zero, and +1 if it is positive. Thus

IF SGN (X) < Ø LET X = −X

SQR (dealt with above) gives square root. SQR X = X ↑ Ø.5. If X is negative an error results. See Program 11.

Finally, a not-function, but I need to put it somewhere. The BBC micro stores the value of π permanently. Get it with PI, and get the value 3.14159265. In fact the value in the machine is (wait for it): 3.14159265331322574 or so. Just in case you wanted to know. (All numbers can be got out of this computer with that precision if necessary.)

DIY FUNCTIONS

As you have seen (if you're still reading this!) there are many useful functions in BBC BASIC (most of the above are provided with most micros of course). But, if you're not satisfied and have some other function you often want worked out—then you can define it and then use it just like the others. I'm going to give only brief details of what to do here. Most readers will not have the need—if *you* do, read these notes and then if necessary turn to the *Manual* (or to a fairly good BASIC textbook).

Step 1

Use DEF FN (define function) to tell the micro what you want. Say you want a function called POWER whose value is given by $x^3 + y^2$. Put in the following, at an address away from the main program:

1ØØØ   DEF FNPOWER (X, Y) = X ↑ 3 + Y ↑ 2

Step 2

Whenever in your program you want to use your function, call the function with FNPOWER (X, Y) or whatever. You don't need to use the same variable names each time—these fragments both work:

1Ø   INPUT "Values □", X, Y

2Ø   PRINT "Power □"; FNPOWER (X, Y)

11Ø   INPUT "Numbers □", A, B

12Ø   PRINT "Result □"; FNPOWER (A, B)

(Note that, despite what the *Manual* says, you don't need to keep your function definitions apart from the main program—they don't interfere at all. It's just administratively more convenient to put them in their own little corner.)

PROJECTS

1. Enter, study, use and understand this program:

Program 12: Factors

```
10  MODE 5: COLOUR 130: COLOUR 1: CLS
20  PRINT TAB (22): "**FACTORIZATION**"
30  PRINT ' ' ' "(To find the factors of an input number)"
40  REPEAT: PRINT ' ' ' "What is the □ □ number?"; : INPUT A
50  IF A < 1 OR A < > INT (A) PRINT "ENTER POSITIVE
    WHOLENUMBER ONLY": FOR W = 1 TO 5000: NEXT: CLS:
    GOTO 40
60  CLS: PRINT "The factors of "; A; ": " ' '
70  FOR B = 1 TO A/2: IF A = B * INT (A/B) PRINT B
80  NEXT: PRINT A
90  C$ = GET$: CLS: UNTIL C$ = "0"
```

Only the last line is a new idea—the program loops until you press 0 after a set of factors has been printed.

2. Now improve Program 12 as you see fit.
3. Or use the ideas in it to print out prime numbers up to the BBC's limit (if you have time . . .). A prime number is one whose only factors are 1 and itself.
4. An object falling from rest moves faster and faster to Earth. (I cheat and ignore air friction.) After t seconds its speed is 10t metres per second and it has fallen 5t metres. Write a BBC program to input time of fall and print out final speed and distance fallen, with suitable messages.
5. (A special for teachers and writers!) The "required reading age" of a piece of text is given by a formula like this:

    $$AGE = 5 + 0.4 \,(w/s + p/w)$$

    Here w is the number of words in the piece; s is the number of sentences; and p is the number of words of more than two syllables. Develop a text analysis program based on this.

10 Getting it Taped

By now, you will have typed a lot of programs into your Beeb, and lost them with NEW or when switching off at three in the morning. By now, indeed, you may well have got around to saving programs on to cassette for loading when you want to impress yourself or your visitors.

The main work in this chapter is, therefore, concerned with "the cassette interface", so that the routines can be set out with any problems noted. Your early exploration of the "Welcome" cassette will have helped you to overcome these barriers:

1. Finding a cassette recorder that works fairly reliably in this context.
2. Finding a suitable lead to connect this to the micro.
3. Getting the hang of LOAD ". . ." and CHAIN ". . .".

If you actually have to buy a cassette recorder, you can of course purchase the "official" BBC one. This is available more cheaply (in some form or another) from a number of suppliers. Otherwise look for the cheapest mono cassette recorder with, if possible, these features:

> remote control
> tape counter
> treble (tone) control

You *can* manage without any of these (I do!), but they certainly help.

LOADING

There are two commands here, LOAD and CHAIN. (There are also the commands *LOAD and *RUN which you may meet with some published software.) Each should be followed by the name of the program to be loaded. The structure LOAD " " (or CHAIN " ") works, but may not be so reliable—use it if you like, to get the next recorded program, whatever it may be, into the computer memory.

You may use such structures as these (with CHAIN instead of LOAD) in each case:

1. LOAD " "   [load the next program found]
2. LOAD "name"   [load the program with that exact name, if found]
3. LOAD A$ [if A$ has been assigned]

LOAD can't be used in a program, so using (3) is a bit unlikely. CHAIN *can* be used in a program, so you can have things like this:

> 50   PRINT "Enter name of program wanted " ' ' "NAME", "CONTENT"

> 60   PRINT ' "1", "Breakout"

```
70  PRINT ' "2", "Asteroid"
80  PRINT ' "3", "Invaders" ' '
90  INPUT P$: CLS: CHAIN P$
```

There are other differences between LOAD and CHAIN. The obvious one is that CHAIN sets the program running straightaway, a bit like LOAD ". . .": RUN (R). Not *quite* the same though—LOAD clears the memory entirely, but CHAIN leaves some data that can be carried through from the old program to the new one. (*Some*, not a lot! But this is an advanced feature . . .)

SAVING PROGRAMS

The command here is SAVE, which *must* be followed by the program name in quotes. (I mean, there are no tricks like SAVE " " and SAVE P$ in this case—they wouldn't be much use anyway!)

The program name must start with a letter or a number and thereafter can have any combination you like of letters, numbers, spaces and keyboard characters. The name can be as long as you like, but obviously long complex names could lead to later problems! (Recall that to LOAD a program by name, the name you use in LOAD "name" *must* be identical to that used when saving.)

If you find you can't re-LOAD programs SAVEd in the "official" way, first listen to the recording by ear. If it is very quiet, very loud, muffled or distorted, or contains any hums or squeaks, you will need to check all aspects of your interface. Some possible problems may be solved by disconnecting the EAR lead during SAVEs (if you can); reducing the volume setting to just above zero; and moving micro and audio equipment away from the TV and the power leads. There's more on this subject coming next.

LOADING PROBLEMS

If you are able to load the "Welcome" programs, but your computer doesn't like your own recordings, try the following tips.

1. Play with the volume control.
2. Keep tone on maximum treble.
3. Move the micro and tape recorder as far from the TV as possible.
4. Make sure that the audio leads do not come close to any leads carrying mains current.
5. Load with the microphone link disconnected (if your machine allows that).

With some early models of the Beeb, overheating problems can make loading and saving erratic or impossible. A major difficulty can be that the saved signal is so bad that the computer can't understand it when trying to load. All sorts of strange messages appear on screen in this case; return the machine for modification.

One way to check for successful saving is to re-wind the tape and enter the command *CAT (= catalogue). This prints up details of all the programs met as the tape runs and will show rubbish if your program hasn't recorded properly. (The main use of *CAT is of course to let you find the names of programs stored on a cassette, but you've written their names on the label, haven't you?)

ERROR MESSAGES

And now for something completely different—or have you been troubled with dire warnings from the Beeb while going through the saving/loading stuff?

It is fairly fair to say that computers can't make mistakes—they follow the instructions given (whether in ROM or typed in from the keyboard). But if they don't understand what you tell them, or you make a typing slip, they'll tell you. Mind you, there are all sorts of errors you don't find out about so easily—the computer understands the instructions, but they're not what you meant.

The *User Guide* gives a list of some "error messages" the Beeb is trained to supply in different circumstances. But there are plenty of others, as you may have found by now. And some versions of the machine get so hot that they really do stop working properly after a while. (This should not happen, of course—and I'm afraid it means sending the thing back.)

Particularly common error reports are as follows:

Mistake You used an unrecognisable command or program statement. (In the latter case the report will tell you the line that needs checking.) For instance,

"run" for "RUN"

or "PR INT" or "PRONT" for "PRINT".

Syntax error You used a recognisable command or program keyword but what followed it doesn't follow the rules. For instance, "LIST A" is not acceptable to the Beeb, even if A has been assigned a value. (Many computers would accept this useful technique.) So the "grammar" or *syntax* of the LIST command has not been obeyed.

In fact syntax errors are so common that many have their own messages. The most frequent ones are discussed, albeit briefly, in the *User Guide*. On the whole the messages are fairly clear, even if it is not always obvious what they're referring to! But I can't help you much more—BBC errors are the subject of a whole book, not just a page. Just one more tip, though. Beeb error messages refer to the error-line if it's in a program—but if your lines are long, it can be a devil of a job pin-pointing the problem. MORAL: Keep your lines short. That's a good moral anyway!

All the same, you should be aware of the useful structure ON ERROR . . . This blocks the usual error routines for the rest of the program, or until it meets ON ERROR OFF. If there is an error of any kind thereafter it is handled as *you* decide. What you decide is rarely likely to be as effective as what BBC decided! The problem is that ON ERROR . . . blocks *all* error routines, so you should replace all of them to be safe. However, I used the technique in Program 11 to block program-stops due to trying to square root a negative number. But what I did would also block reports of any other possible error made.

11 Coming to a Decision

Right at the beginning of this book I went on about the fact that computers are able to carry out millions of actions in a second. The point then was (mainly) that this makes essential the "stored program" concept.

Now it is time to think about decisions—the single most important aspect of any programming system. There are two kinds of decision as far as we're concerned. Both make computers very powerful and yet easy to program. Both allow the micro to carry out many actions without too many instructions. I'll call these two kinds "implied" decisions and "open" decisions. (I made the words up, but I'm not alone in thinking the idea important.)

Without knowing it (I guess) you're very much used to *implied decisions*. They are needed in the *loop* structures given by the BBC's FOR . . . NEXT and REPEAT . . . UNTIL. Compare these two program fragments. Can you see that each expects (implies) that the micro can make decisions?

FOR A = 1 TO 1000	A = 0: REPEAT: A = A + 1
(do such and such)	(do such and such)
NEXT A	UNTIL A = 1000
(do something else)	(do something else)

You can see both structures in Figure 11.1 overleaf, it's very like the one on page 33.

The decision part, in the diamond-shaped box, is essential. What the computer does is:

1. Assign the starting value to variable A.
2. Increase the value by 1 (increment it by 1).
3. Do such and such.
4. Test whether A has reached 1000:
    (a) If not (FALSE) go back to step (2);
    (b) If so (TRUE) go on to do something else.

Each time round the loop, then, the computer carries out a test; the result of the test decides what happens next. The need for test + decision is implied in the loop structures FOR . . . NEXT and REPEAT . . . UNTIL (and the WHILE . . . DO you may meet with other micros).

Here's a third program fragment that has just the same effect. This time the decision is not implied—it is out in the open. That's why I call it an *open decision*. We have met a number of examples of its main structure, IF . . . THEN, already.

    100   A = 0

    110   A = A + 1

    120   do such and such

51

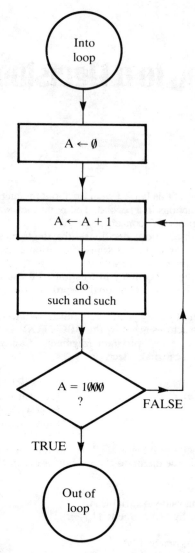

Figure 11.1

130   IF A < 1000 THEN GOTO 110

140   do something else

I hope you can see several things here. First, do you agree that it is in effect just the same as before? That, in other words, the diagram above describes it? What *this* approach does is simply bring the decision out into the open.

Something else different may be slightly less obvious—I've had to use line-numbers. This is because of the GOTO statement—it has to know where to go. Programs without GOTOs and line-numbers are much "nicer" than ones with. Unfortunately BBC BASIC has a line-number structure and there's nothing we can do about it.

IF . . . THEN

We can use this open decision structure in many more cases than just for looping. (In fact, why use it for looping? REPEAT . . . UNTIL and FOR . . . NEXT are much better!) It is, as I've said, very powerful and one of BASIC's most valuable structures. Here's how it works:

IF (something if true)   THEN (do this)   otherwise don't.

As soon as the computer gets to the IF, it carries out the test "is something (whatever it is) true?". IF it is THEN it carries out the next instruction. IF not THEN it doesn't.

Three points increase the power of this concept in the case of the BBC (and some other BASICs).

1. We can cater for the "otherwise" situation using the keyword ELSE. IF (something is true) THEN (go here) ELSE (go there). Thus:

    IF SCORE = 10 THEN GOTO 500 ELSE GOTO 600

2. The THEN doesn't have to have a GOTO after it: any keyword can do:

    IF SCORE = 10 THEN PRINT "Excellent!" ELSE PRINT "Keep trying!"

3. The multi-statement approach works, using colons:

    IF SCORE = 10 THEN PRINT "Excellent!": BONUS = BONUS + 1
                   ELSE PRINT "Keep trying!": IF BONUS > 1 THEN
                   BONUS = BONUS − 1

We don't need that line of spaces in that last example; I put them in to make what's going on clearer. *It is very easy to become confused in IF . . . lines.* Figure 11.2 shows what that last line does, see over the page.

Please take great care with IF . . . lines. Otherwise you'll spend ages trying to find out why your precious program doesn't work properly. You have been warned!

To make matters worse, you don't actually need the THEN in BBC BASIC, but there *must* be a space:

IF A > B   A = B   ELSE B = A

Confusing, yes? To make matters still worse you don't need a GOTO before a line-number in IF . . . statements:

IF A > B THEN 600   [this is an "implied" GOTO]

But you can't write

IF A > B 600

or

IF A > B PRINT "Bigger": 600

I'm really telling you all these last points so that you can recognise them in program listings. I'd strongly advise you always to use THEN and GOTO in your own programs— it makes them easier to read, less open to error and less hard to check. And here's a final, *very* important warning . . .

This works:

100   IF A$ = "CAT" THEN PRINT "Good"

110   PRINT ′ "Now try the next one."

Whatever the value of A$, the message "Now try . . ." appears. *This* looks as if it should do the same:

100   IF A$ = "CAT" THEN PRINT "Good": PRINT " Now try the next one."

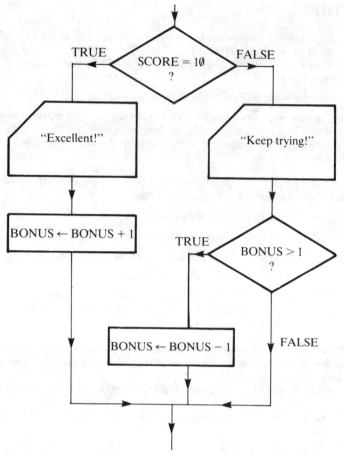

Figure 11.2

But the message comes on screen *only* if A$ = "CAT".

The colon multi-statement idea needs special care in IF lines. This is because in such a line, this is what the computer does.

1. Carry out the test after IF.
   (a) If the test gives a TRUE answer, then carry out all statements until an ELSE appears . . .
   (b) If the test gives a FALSE answer, scan the line for an ELSE, then carry out all statements after it . . .
2. Go to next line.

So—to repeat, yet again, *it is very easy to become confused in IF . . . lines!*

The following program should help you to understand the versatility—and dangers— of IF. Enter it, try to predict the outcome of different values of A, and see if you're right. And if you're really keen, try to draw a diagram of it like those earlier in this section . . .

Program 13: IF what?

```
10   A = INT (RND (5))
20   IF A = 1 THEN PRINT 1
```

```
30    IF A = 1 THEN GOTO 10
40    IF A = 2 THEN PRINT 25
50    IF A = 2 THEN CLS
60    IF A < 3 THEN PRINT A * 100
70    IF A = 3 THEN PRINT "A = 3"
80    IF A > 2 THEN IF A < 5 THEN FOR B = 1 TO 1000: NEXT B
90    IF A * A < 20 THEN PRINT A; "SQUARED IS □"; A * A
100   IF A = 4 THEN PRINT PI
110   IF A = 4 THEN GOTO 10
120   IF A < 3 THEN STOP
130   IF A = 5 PRINT A; "MESS"
140   GOTO 10
```

MORE IFS AND BUTS

Quite often we need an IF . . . THEN IF . . . structure. "IF it is raining THEN IF I have an umbrella THEN I'll use it ELSE I'll take shelter." The same is true of computing as of real life—"IF the score is ten THEN IF there've been ten goes THEN congratulate ELSE give more practice." Sometimes we need even more complexity—IF . . . THEN IF . . . THEN IF . . . THEN . . . and so on. I shan't try to give an example; I'm sure you take the point.

We can re-word the raining sentence like this. "IF it is raining AND I have an umbrella THEN I'll use it ELSE I'll take shelter." And we can do the same in BASIC. But I hope you can already see dangers—which IF does the ELSE refer to? I'll come back to that, but be warned in advance.

"IF the score is ten AND there've been ten goes THEN congratulate . . . and so on."

The AND here is a useful keyword (strictly it's called a *logical operator*). Here's what the line would actually look like:

IF SCORE = 10 AND GOES = 10 THEN PRINT "Full marks" ELSE PRINT "Here's another one!": GOTO somewhere

Take a look at Program A3 (at the end of the book); this shows how this AND business works in a sort of game. I *could* have put all the IFs into one complex IF . . . THEN . . . ELSE etc. etc. line, but it *would* have been complex, wouldn't it?

Another logical operator of value here is OR. With care (again!) you can compare it to the English "or"—IF it is raining OR if it is snowing AND I have an umbrella THEN I'll use it ELSE I'll take shelter. So—in BASIC:

IF SCORE = 10 OR SCORE = 9 AND GOES = 10 THEN PRINT "A good score" ELSE . . . and so on.

But you *can* see the rocks of complexity again, can't you? Fortunately we can use brackets to ensure the right priority for the computer:

IF (SCORE = 10 OR SCORE = 9) AND GOES = 10 THEN . . .

or even (to be completely sure)

IF ((SCORE = 10 OR SCORE = 9) AND GOES = 10) THEN . . .

Structures like this that use only one IF do not lead to the ELSE problem I mentioned above—if there's only one IF then the ELSE must apply to it. If there's more than one IF, the ELSE applies to the *last* one. (Indeed you can nest them: IF this THEN IF that THEN such and such ELSE so and so ELSE the other. But *how* complex!)

CONCLUSION

IF is *very* important, and in BBC BASIC is very flexible. However the flexibility leads to all kinds of possible dangers—TAKE GREAT CARE WITH IF!!

IF you're human, THEN you're by now probably getting a bit lazy with the projects in these pages. But please take some time over the ones that now follow, ELSE you're likely to have many problems in future . . .

PROJECTS

1. Draw the detailed flowchart section that would show these program lines:

```
100  INPUT ANSWER$
110  IF ANSWER$ = "brown" THEN BROWN = BROWN + 1 ELSE
     IF ANSWER$ = "red" THEN RED = RED + 1 ELSE
     IF ANSWER$ = "white" THEN BROWN = BROWN + 1:
     RED = RED + 1 ELSE PRINT "Only brown, red or white please!":
     GOTO 100
120  PRINT ' "Brown", BROWN ' "Red", RED ' "White", BROWN + RED
```

2. Code the loop shown below in three different BBC BASIC ways.
3. Write your own program like (but better than!) Program 13.

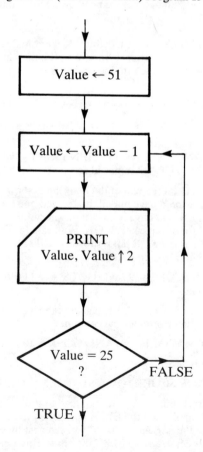

Figure 11.3

12 Picturing Programs

In the previous chapter, in which I delved into decisions, the need became urgent for showing what's going on in pictorial form. The kind of diagram I used to show the action of various structures has also appeared earlier in the book—it is called a *flowchart*.

It is as important for a programmer to be able to devise and to read flowcharts as it is for an electrician to deal in circuit diagrams. In fact the concepts are very much the same. In both cases:

1. The diagram lets one see very quickly what's going on.
2. The diagram is easier to check than the actual creation (circuit or program).
3. The diagram is fairly universally understandable.

Compare the circuit diagram in Figure 12.1 with the actual circuit beside it. Which better shows the viewer the structure?

In just the same way the symbolic London Underground map is much easier to use than a real one would be. And in just the same way a flowchart shows structure much better than a BASIC listing.

Flowcharting is very simple. All you need to know is the set of symbols used and rules to be followed. (Mind you, I must admit that the language of flowcharting suffers a bit from dialect problems!) Anyway, here is the concept as much as we need to know it.

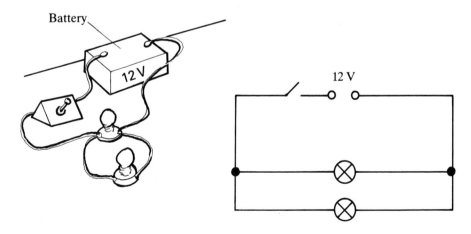

Figure 12.1

THE LANGUAGE OF FLOWCHARTING

I shall set out symbols and rules together. Here goes.

Rule 1   A flowchart must have one beginning and (preferably only) one end.
SYMBOLS—the START and STOP "boxes" are shown in Figure 12.2.

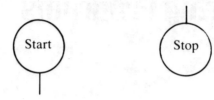

Figure 12.2

Rule 2   The direction of flow in a chart is from START at the top to STOP at the
bottom. The normal direction of horizontal flow is to the right. Use arrows
for all other directions.
SYMBOLS—boxes are joined by straight lines, with arrows *at least* where
normal directions are not followed. See Figure 12.3.

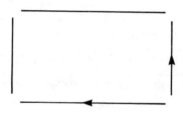

Figure 12.3

Notes: I think it wise to use more arrows than the minimum. Also if a chart
covers more than one sheet of paper, use connector boxes like those shown in
Figure 12.4.

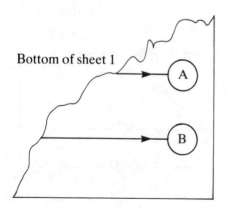
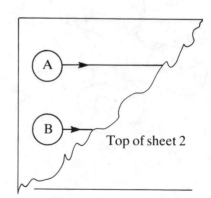

Figure 12.4

Rule 3   Show each stage in the structure with a box in the flowchart.
SYMBOLS—we need boxes to show INPUT, OUTPUT, DECISION and
any other kind of ACTION. They are shown in Figure 12.5.
Notes: These symbols are where some people differ! Also there are plenty
more special symbols that posh folk in industry and commerce may use, but
this is quite enough to get by on.

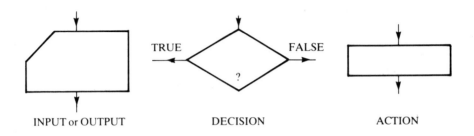

| INPUT or OUTPUT | DECISION | ACTION |

Figure 12.5

And that's it. Easy, n'est-ce pas?

When I teach physics (which is officially my job . . .) and get on to circuit diagrams, I give practice in two ways. Firstly, given a circuit description, prepare a diagram; secondly, given a diagram, prepare a circuit. Students need to be very familiar with circuit diagrams. And it's just as true of flowcharts. They are very useful indeed—so there are some projects on them at the end of this chapter. But in what ways *are* they so very useful?

USING FLOWCHARTS

It used to be traditional (I mean, a couple of years ago!) to expect programmers to develop flowcharts before starting to write the program itself. There would then be two stages. The *outline flowchart* would show, in only a page or two, the broad stages of the project. Then a *detailed flowchart* would set out what the program would do almost line by line.

Nowadays, like many other teachers, I feel that there is no real need for detailed flowcharts. The program itself should be so well laid out that it would be quite clear.

Some folk go further and suggest that the outline flowchart should be drawn *after* the program is finished rather than before it starts. But I don't agree with that. I advise you *always* to put your ideas down as an outline flowchart before starting work on anything more than a very simple program. It doesn't need to be beautifully neat, but it *does* need to be clear.

DOCUMENTATION

And now we come to another important piece of advice. It is that you *keep adequate records of your programs!* By this time you are probably beginning to build up a fairly extensive library of BBC program cassettes. Get organized now!

1. Do not keep more than four lengthy programs on one cassette (two on each side). Make and keep second copies of anything you'd hate to lose.
2. Number the cassettes (whether they're ones you've recorded or ones you've bought). Code duplicates as (a) and (b). Thus

    5a BEEB INVADERS—master copy   5b—copy for daily use

3. Buy a loose-leaf file and keep in it an index plus, in number order, all the papers associated with each cassette.
4. Store the cassettes neatly, in number order, and keep the file near them. (The cassettes should not be exposed to direct sun, high or low temperatures, dust or magnetic-fields.) Look again at the picture on Page 6!

If you start such a system now, when you have only a few cassettes, you'll be glad of it when you have dozens. (I learned the hard way, but what I've described is what I do with the several hundred program cassettes I have.)

Anyway what about this paper-work in the file, this *documentation*? You've got to provide for two situations, so there are two kinds of documentation—user document-ation and programmer documentation.

User documentation

User documentation includes everything associated with a program that helps anyone using it to run it without problems. It is, in other words, the instructions.

I think that the only instructions for the user (of anything but a complex program) should be how to load it—though a description of one or two lines in the index is obviously needed. Everything else should be in the program itself. Use lines like this:

```
50  PRINT ' "This program does such and such"
```

or

```
50  PRINT ' "This is a game where you have to do so and so"
60  INPUT ' ' ' "Do you want INSTRUCTIONS (Y or N)", A$
70  IF A$ = "Y" OR A$ = "y" THEN GOTO 5000
80  [get on with the program]
       . . . . .
4990  STOP
5000  CLS: PRINT ' ' ' "Here is what you do . . ."
       . . . . .
5090  CLS: GOTO 80
```

There are two major advantages of putting user instructions into the program like that. Number 1—no bits of paper to lose. And Number 2—it'll force you to keep the instructions simple, short and clear!

Programmer documentation

Now for something completely different. What *this* kind of documentation has to do is help you (or someone else) to improve the program in the future. What do you mean?—"my programs can't be improved." Wrong!—just you wait and see. For a start, each user will (unless shy) give you extra ideas. And then, in a few months, your growing experience will show you new and better ways to do things. *Programmer documentation makes later improvement easy.* To some extent you can put this kind of information in the program. BASIC has the useful REM (= remark) statement just for this purpose. Any line starting with REM appears when you LIST, but is ignored when you RUN. Let me add REMs to the last program fragment to show what I mean:

```
10  REMARKABLE GAME BY ABDUL SMITH JULY 1982!!!
49  REM introduction
50  PRINT ' "This program does such and such."
60  INPUT ' ' ' "Do you want INSTRUCTIONS (Y or N)", A$
```

```
69    REM A$ is Y/N answer. Y sends control to line 5000.
      All other values are ignored.
70    IF A$ = "Y" or A$ = "y" THEN GOTO 5000
78    REM *** PROGRAM START ***
79    REM ===================
80    . . . . .
4989  REMember to delete next line
4990  STOP
4999  REM instructions
5000  CLS: PRINT ' "Here is what you do . . ."
      . . . . .
5089  REM—Return to main program
5090  CLS: GOTO 80
```

Fine. Well, that's all clear now. So why not just use REMs?—Why bother with paper that's likely to get lost?

In short, you *needn't* bother—with *simple* programs. But if your program is more than a few dozen lines you *do* need paper. After all, an adequate number of REMs will take up quite a lot of memory and also increase SAVE/LOAD times. And it's not easy to use them when they're scattered through a number of screens of listing. So, think about keeping the following in your paper file:

1. Program name, length, date, author, cassette number(s).
2. Program description, and source of idea.
3. List of all variables used, with their meanings and any comments.
4. Outline flowchart with, added, the line-numbers covered by each box.
5. Notes of any special tricks you used.
6. Date and details of later amendments.
7. Ideas for future development.

Do all that nicely (even if not very neatly) and one day you may be able to add:

8. Date and place of publication; price!

PROJECTS

1. Choose two or three of the programs earlier in this book and one of the simpler ones at the end—and prepare a careful outline flowchart. Programs 13 and A3 are *real* tests! (Keep your answers, by the way.)
2. Study the flowchart in Figure 12.6 overleaf and then describe the idea in words.
3. . . . and then, if you're keen, write a program to express it.
4. Add REMs to one or two of your own programs and try to work out how many there *should* be.
5. Prepare a full two sheets of program documentation for one of your less simple programs.
6. Try to write a program based on one of your answers to question (1). Compare the result to the original and decide how good your flowcharting is!
7. Organize your software collection as I've suggested, including the file, before it's too late . . .

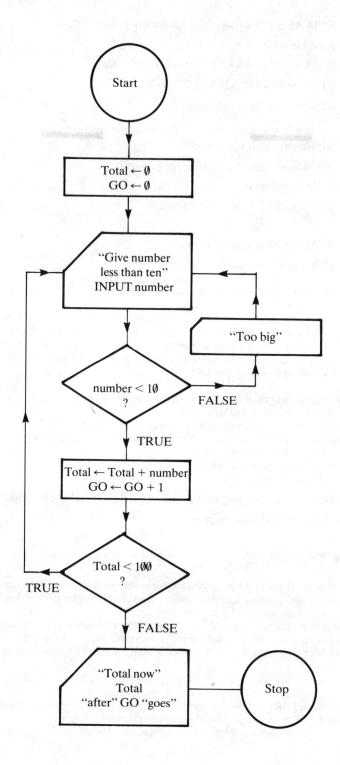

Figure 12.6

13 Proceeding Along

Now that our BBC programs include decision-making, they gain a more complex structure. (And that's why I took time off just now to look at flowcharting.) BBC BASIC offers two facilities for keeping things simple in the more advanced programs we can now work on. The word *subroutine* covers both.

A subroutine is any section of a program (routine) which has a clear single purpose. I want to explore the background theory in more detail in the next chapter, so let me just give a summary now.

The most efficient way of developing a program is to break the initial concept down into a number of chunks. (Recall the outline flowchart?) Each chunk (or *module*) has one function and can be coded into a subroutine in the program as a whole. If that's not clear, take a look at Figure 13.1. Each box shows a module.

So that's subroutines then—chunks of a complete program each with their own job to do. What most folk mean by subroutines are chunks that appear separate in the listing from the main program stream. The sketch shows this (Figure 13.2). What the main program then does is to "call" on a given subroutine whenever it's needed. We describe such subroutines as *closed*.

This approach has two advantages. The first is obvious—in a program of much length you are likely to find that the same module has to be used several times (SUB A in Figure 13.2). Then it need appear only once in the listing, yet be called as often as it's wanted. The second is less obvious. It is that the lines of a subroutine are particularly easy to check and correct, without involving the main program. This can save a huge amount of time and trouble.

GOSUB . . . RETURN

I said BBC BASIC has two ways of giving closed subroutines. First I'd like to discuss the one that's standard to all BASICs. (Because the Beeb has a non-standard one too, the way it deals with this one is not very advanced.)

There are two new keywords here. To call up a subroutine, use GOSUB n, where n is the first line of the subroutine. To tell the micro that the subroutine is finished, use RETURN. Command then goes back to the line after that GOSUB. This is shown more clearly in Figure 13.3.

When the computer meets GOSUB n it stores in memory its current position in the program, and then goes off to line n. When the computer meets RETURN it fishes around in memory to find where to return to, and back it comes. Just like using a bookmark to keep your place while you're looking at the pictures in the middle.

The section of memory that stores the current position can get pretty busy. This is because you can "nest" subroutines as much as you like—a sub can call a second which can call a third and so on. Just as with nested IF statements, though, things can get tricky in practice—you need to take care.

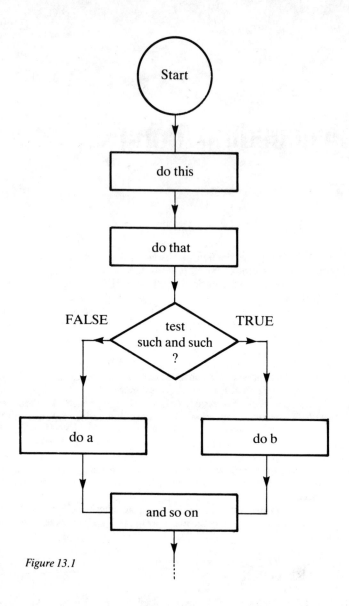

Figure 13.1

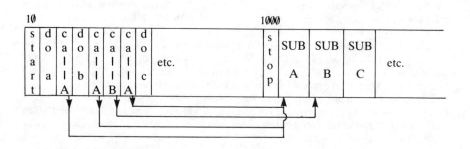

Figure 13.2

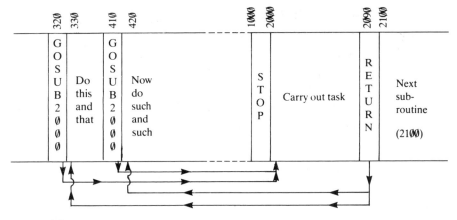

Figure 13.3

It's a useful structure, the closed subroutine. Get used to it, especially when your programs need the same lines time and time again. Program 14 is an example. Study it! I've put a sketch of the flows of command after the listing (Figure 13.4).

Program 14: Screen fill

1∅	MODE 5: COLOUR 129: COLOUR 3	
2∅	GOSUB 4∅∅	[call "wait" subroutine]
3∅	PRINT ' "□ Enter one letter & RETURN"	
4∅	INPUT ' ' ' A$	[a useful trick here!]
5∅	GOSUB 3∅∅	[call "fill" subroutine]
6∅	GOSUB 4∅∅	[and "wait" again]
7∅	PRINT ' "□ What's your name?"	
8∅	INPUT ' ' ' N$	
9∅	LET A$ = N$	
1∅∅	GOSUB 3∅∅	
11∅	GOSUB 4∅∅	
12∅	PRINT ' "□ Now give any set of characters you like!"	
13∅	INPUT ' ' ' A$	
14∅	GOSUB 3∅∅	
15∅	GOSUB 4∅∅	
16∅	LET A$ = "Thanks, □" + N$	[adding strings]
17∅	REPEAT: GOSUB 3∅∅: GOSUB 4∅∅: UNTIL FALSE	[no end to this!]
18∅	STOP	[not really needed]
3∅∅	CLS	[Here's "fill"]
31∅	FOR A = 1 TO 64∅ / LEN A$: PRINT A$;: NEXT	[LEN A$ = its number of characters]
32∅	GOSUB 4∅∅	[a "nested" subroutine]
33∅	RETURN	[back to main program]

65

400	FOR A = 1 TO 5000: NEXT	[and here's "wait"]
410	CLS	
420	RETURN	[back to main program]

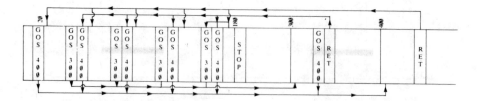

Figure 13.4

Here are some points about the GOSUB . . . RETURN business that you should note.

1. You cannot use structures like this in BBC BASIC: INPUT "Give a number between 1 and 4", A: GOSUB A ∗ 100 followed by relevant subroutines (each with RETURN) at lines 100, 200, 300 and 400.
2. The keyword ON can give this effect, however: INPUT "Give a number between 1 and 4", A: ON A GOSUB 100, 200, 300, 400. Here if A is 1, we go to 100; if it is 2, we go to 200, and so on. Careful trapping is needed, to avoid problems if A ≠ 1, 2, 3 or 4.
3. You can enter a subroutine in the middle if you have the need. Follow this fragment through.

> 20 INPUT "Give a number between 1 and 4", A: IF A < > INT (A)
>
> THEN GOSUB 100 ELSE GOSUB 140
>
> . . . . .
>
> 100 PRINT "I can work only with whole numbers."
>
> 110 PRINT ' "You gave the value □"; A;
>
> 120 A = INT (A + 0.5)
>
> 130 PRINT "□ so I shall take it as □"; A; "."
>
> 140 REM here starts main part of subroutine
>
> . . . . .
>
> 200 RETURN

Did you follow? The subroutine *really* starts at 100, but the first lines deal specially with cases where the user didn't enter a whole number. If he or she *does* enter a whole number we don't want to use those lines, so we GOSUB straight to 140. This is a useful trick.

4. Keep your closed subroutines well away from the main program. The best plan is to put them after line 5000 (say) with STOP at line 4990 to prevent accidental entry.

There's one rather advanced point here, though—the higher a subroutine's starting line-number, the longer it takes for the routine to be found. So if you want highest speed, you can do this instead:

> 10 GOTO 1000
>
> 10–990 subroutines
>
> 1000 start main program.

OK? Let me summarize what we've had so far.

1. A subroutine is a section of a program with a single function.
2. A closed subroutine is one kept apart from the main program, called when needed by GOSUB n and closed by RETURN.
3. The main use of a closed subroutine is to carry out repeated tasks without having to repeat the program lines.

Straightforward! But now let's look at the BEEB's second closed subroutine structure, the "procedure".

PROCEDURES

We can use procedures exactly like subroutines. Here are the differences.

1. Refer to a procedure by name rather than by line-number.
2. Call the procedure with PROCname (no space) instead of GOSUB n.
3. Start the procedure with DEF PROCname (using this spacing).
4. Close the procedure with ENDPROC instead of RETURN.

That can all best be shown by an example—so here is Program 14 using procedures rather than subroutines. Exactly the same diagram would apply to it.

Program 15: Screen fill again!

```
 10   MODE 5: COLOUR 129: COLOUR 3
 20   PROCWAIT                          [call "wait" procedure]
 30   PRINT ' "□ Enter one letter & RETURN"
 40   INPUT ' ' ' A$
 50   PROCFILL (A$)                      [call "fill" procedure]
 60   PROCWAIT                          [and "wait" again]
 70   PRINT ' "□ What's your name?"
 80   INPUT ' ' ' N$
100   PROCFILL (N$)
110   PROCWAIT
120   PRINT ' "Now give any set of characters you like!"
130   INPUT ' ' ' C$
140   PROCFILL (C$)
150   PROCWAIT
170   REPEAT: PROCFILL ("Thanks, □" + N$): PROCWAIT:
      UNTIL FALSE
180   STOP
300   DEF PROCFILL (F$)                  [here's "fill"]
305   CLS
310   FOR A = 1 TO 640 / LEN F$: PRINT F$;: NEXT
320   PROCWAIT                          [a "nested" procedure]
330   ENDPROC
400   DEF PROCWAIT                       [and here's "wait"]
405   FOR A = 1 TO 5000: NEXT
```

```
410   CLS
420   ENDPROC
```

If you compare the bits in Programs 14 and 15 to do with closed subroutines, you'll see that the procedures approach is more complex. So why use it?

There are two reasons. The first I've pointed out already. In BBC BASIC, GOSUB must be followed by *a* line-number while PROC must be followed by a name. So using procedures let's name the closed subroutines. That's useful both when writing programs and when reading them. (Some BASICs allow GOSUB name, mind you, but the Beeb does so only with a struggle.)

The second reason is more advanced; it's to do with how variables are treated in the main program and procedures. I'm not going to say much about it because this *is* advanced, but let's take a little look. Check with Programs 14 and 15 to see what I mean in practice. In the GOSUB approach you must:

1.   Define all the variables you're going to need before going to the subroutine.
2.   Make sure that any other variables used in the subroutine have different names from those in the main program.

Both these restrict the use of GOSUB a lot—but both restrictions are less severe in the procedures approach. Look at this set of program fragments, using GOSUB and PROC respectively.

GOSUB	PROC
50 A = 10: B = 20: C = 14 -	50 C = 14
60 GOSUB 500	60 PROCRESULT (10, 20)
. . . . .	. . . . .
100 INPUT "X, Y values"; X, Y	100 INPUT "X, Y values"; X, Y
110 A = X: B = Y	
120 GOSUB 500	120 PROCRESULT (X, Y)
. . . . .	. . . . .
490 STOP	490 STOP
500 REM Subroutine	500 DEF PROCRESULT (A, B): LOCAL C
510 FOR D = 1 TO 10	510 FOR C = 1 TO 10
520 PRINT D, (A↑2 + B↑3) * D	520 PRINT C, (A↑2 + B↑3) * C
530 NEXT D	530 NEXT C
540 RETURN	540 ENDPROC

I know this is a bit artificial but the main program each time needs the variable C and needs to call on the subroutine with various values of A and B.

As I said before, in the GOSUB approach, you must:

1.   Define all the variables before using the subroutine (lines 50 and 110).
2.   Make sure the other subroutine variables differ from those in the main program (here we need the extra variable D).

Procedures may be a bit more complex, but . . .

1.   Variable values can be passed directly by putting them in brackets after the procedure name (lines 60 and 120).
2.   Other subroutine variables, if defined as LOCAL (line 500), will not interfere with those in the main program.

OK, procedures *are* more advanced than using GOSUBs—but they *are* more flexible and I suggest you get used to them from the start. Here then is a statement of their use extended from the one on page 66.

1. Refer to a procedure by name rather than by line-number. The name may include, in brackets, the variables to be passed between main program and procedure. Thus RESULT (A, B).
2. Call the procedure with PROCname, with, in brackets, the current values of the variables to be passed. Thus PROCRESULT (VALUE, VALUE * 3) or PROCRESULT (5, 24)
3. Start the procedure with DEF PROCname, with, in brackets, the subroutine's names of the variables passed:

    DEF PROCRESULT (P, Q)

    Then tell the computer about variables only to be used in the subroutine:

    LOCAL A, SQUARE

4. Close the procedure with ENDPROC.

SUBs are simple; PROCs are powerful. Use the latter even when your needs are simple!

PROJECTS

1. Write a BASIC program to fill the screen with the user's name in the colour of his/her choice on a background of chosen colour. Write the program twice—once using GOSUB and once using PROC; compare the results.
2. Study the programs listed at the end of the book which use GOSUBs or procedures. Make sure you understand how and why they are used. Draw a memory map with command flow lines (like that on page 66) for one of the simpler ones.
3. You can animate pictures like this.

```
 10   VDU 23, 225 etc.
 50   LET A$ = "□ □ □" + CHR$ (225) + CHR$ (226) + CHR$ (227)
 60   FOR PLACE = 0 TO 13              [in MODE 5]
 70   PROCPRINT
 80   NEXT PLACE
 90   CLS: GOTO 60
100   DEF PROCPLACE
110   PRINT TAB (PLACE, 15); A$
120   ENDPROC
```

Try this simple example (and look at Program A2) and make up more sophisticated routines of your own.

14 Let's Take it from the Top

I've been leading up to this for a long time—a few pages on program design. The ideas here become more and more important the longer your programs. I don't think you can afford to ignore them (unless you have lots of spare time and enjoy frustration) as soon as your programs start to pass the thirty-line mark.

Not even the world's best programmer will be able to write a program of more than twenty or thirty lines without some sort of plan. So it's time for us—*not* the world's best—to talk about planning.

PLANNING

This involves two concepts that I've already introduced—the concepts of flowcharts and modules. I hope you'll recall that a *flowchart* is a diagram showing how the different parts of a program relate, and each of those parts is a *module*, a section with a single clear function. A third concept we've met is the *subroutine*—a program section that corresponds to a flowchart box.

So here are the stages of development of a program, set out using those words.

Step 1   Have an idea . . .
        THEN break it down into concepts—modules.
Step 2   Design the outline flowchart . . .
        Each box relates to a module.
Step 3   Write the program . . .
        Each subroutine relates to a flowchart box.

The alternative looks much simpler:

Step 1   Have an idea
Step 2   Write the program

Please don't be tempted by that! Programming is not like writing a letter to a friend—the result must be very precise in the way it carries out its task. In a letter to a friend you can get away with things like "Oh, by the way" and "I forgot to say that" and "PS"—in a program you can't.

Let me show you what I mean, by developing a simple program in these three stages. It *has* to be a simple program, because I'm short of space—so it *has* to be rather trivial. Still that'll make it easier for me to show what I'm talking about . . .

IDEA TO MODULES

This is Step 1—have an idea and break it down into modules.

Idea   "I'd like a program that prints two input numbers in order and also gives the mean (average)."

That statement already has some obvious concepts in it:

Concepts 1 (a) Accept two numbers.
     (b) Print them in order.
     (c) Print their mean.

That would be quite enough if we were giving instructions to a person—but micros aren't so clever, so we must be more precise:

Concepts 2 (a) Ask for two numbers.
     (b) Accept two numbers; reject other inputs and re-start.
     (c) If the numbers aren't in order, put them in order.
     (d) Print the two numbers.
     (e) Work out the mean; print it.

That's much more precise now. But in practice we want a program to keep restarting until told to stop. And in practice, a program must help the user as much as possible. (It must be "user-friendly.")

The restart-until-told-to-stop is best handled with what folk call a "rogue value". When the micro comes across this it knows it needn't go on. Let's use the letter "S" for this purpose. Taking the rogue value and the user-friendly thing gives us this final list of concepts. I'll now call them modules.

Idea   A program to print two input numbers in order and give their mean.
Modules (a) Ask for two numbers.
     (b) If input is "S", stop with suitable message.
     (c) Accept two numbers; reject (politely) other inputs and re-start.
     (d) If the numbers aren't in order, put them in order.
     (e) Print the two numbers with suitable message.
     (f) Work out the mean; print it with suitable message.
     (g) Re-start.

MODULES TO FLOWCHART BOXES

Step 2 is very easy—we just have to express the list of modules as a picture—a flowchart. This will show clearly the exact lines of flow through the program (see Figure 14.1).

Drawing up the flowchart, and coding the program, may show the need for other modules in practice. Program development is often much less precise than my three steps imply!

CODING

Writing the program itself should now be (almost) a doddle. The only worries are how to code each stage, for we know that the stages relate to each other correctly.

All we need to do is to write the program lines for each module/flowchart box, either as an open subroutine (part of the main program) or as a closed subroutine (a separate chunk). We can test as we go along.

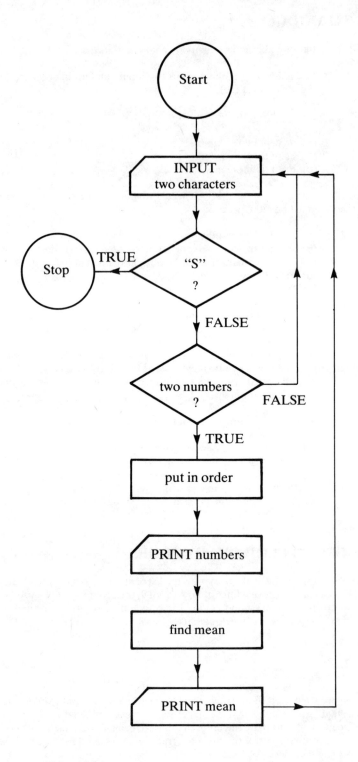

Figure 14.1

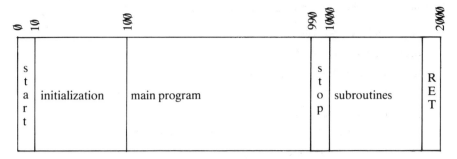

Figure 14.2

Before we start coding we need to lay out a "memory map" of the program. This can often be fairly complex, with several separate blocks of closed subroutines. In our case, that's not needed, so our map is simple, as shown in Figure 14.2. The main program starts at line 100, after any "initialization" (= start up) lines we may decide to include. The subroutines start at 1000.

Here's our starting program skeleton then:

Program 16: Numbers (under development)

9	REM ** INITIALIZATION **	[it's useful to end REMs with 9]
10	MODE 5: CLS	
99	REM ** MAIN PROGRAM **	
990	STOP	[separate subroutines]
999	REM ** SUBROUTINES **	
1990	ENDPROC	[in case you forget]

Do use *KEY 10 "OLD ¦ M LIST ¦ M " and *KEY 0 "RUN ¦ M" of course!

And now, module by module, off we go . . .

Module (a)   Ask for two numbers.

100   PRINT ' "□ □ □ Please enter two numbers or S to stop."
110   PRINT ' "□ □ □ Press RETURN after each answer." ' ' '

Module (b)   If input is "S", stop with suitable message.

120	INPUT A$, B$	[strings can be numbers]
130	IF A$ = "S" OR A$ = "s" OR B$ = "S" OR B$ = "s" THEN PROCSTOP	
1000	DEF PROCSTOP: LOCAL A$	[the first closed subroutine]
1010	CLS: PRINT ' "You entered 'S' —doyou want to stop?"	[no space]
1020	PRINT ' "Please enter Y or N and RETURN."	
1030	INPUT A$: IF A$ = "Y"OR A$ = "y" THEN PRINT ' ' ' "Thank-you!" '	
	"To start again, typeRUN and RETURN." ' ' ':STOP	[no space]
1040	ENDPROC	

73

Module (c)   Accept two numbers; reject (politely) other inputs and re-start.

```
140  PROCCHECK
1050  DEF PROCCHECK
1060  FLAG = 0: A = VAL (A$):
      B = VAL (B$)                    [see below]
1070  IF A = 0 AND A$ < > "0"
      THEN FLAG = 1                   [see below]
1080  IF B = 0 AND B$ < > "0"
      THEN FLAG = 1
1090  ENDPROC
150  IF FLAG = 1 PRINT ' ' "Not valid numbers:" ' "Please re-enter!":
      FOR WAIT = 1 TO 2000: NEXT: GOTO 120
```

I said "see below" because line 1060 needs comment. It introduces a new *string function*, called VAL. What VAL (string) does is to turn the string (a collection of any kind of characters) into a number. If the string contains any characters other than number ones (full stop in particular) the result of VAL is 0.

So in line 1060 A = VAL (A$) tries to turn A$ into a number. If it fails A gets to be 0. However A will also get to be 0 if A$ is "0"—that's why 1070 has that AND in it. Same with B and B$ in lines 1060 and 1080.

1060 also introduces a variable I've called FLAG. I used the name on purpose—by the word "flag" computer folk mean a variable whose value is 0 or 1 depending whether something is false or true. So the value of FLAG in this program tells us whether the inputs are OK numbers (FLAG = 0) or not (FLAG = 1). Line 150 then takes re-start action if necessary. I hope it's polite enough for you!

Module (d)   If the numbers aren't in order, put them in order.

Module (e)   Print the two numbers with suitable message.

As Module (d) is so easy with only two numbers, I put the two modules together:

```
160  PROCORDER
1100  DEF PROCORDER
1110  CLS: PRINT ' ' "Your two numbers are" ' '
1120  IF A < B PRINT A, B ELSE PRINT B, A
1130  ENDPROC
```

Module (f)   Work out the mean, print it with suitable message. Home straight now . . .

```
170  PRINT ' ' ' "Mean—": (A + B) / 2
```

. . . and straight home:

Module (g)   Re-start

```
180  PRINT TAB (0, 20); "Please press RETURN to re-start . . ."
190  R = GET: GOTO 100
```

Note a useful trick there—R = GET in line 190 causes the computer to stop and wait till a key is pressed. Very useful indeed!

That's now a good implementation of the original idea (even if the original idea wasn't such a good one). It can be improved, I'm sure, and it can easily be made more complex. But it appears here as a demo of developing programs. Remember? Remember!

The posh name for this kind of program development is modular, or *top-down programming*, hence the title of this chapter. I can easily sketch the approach like the diagram in Figure 14.3; then the reason for the name is clear.

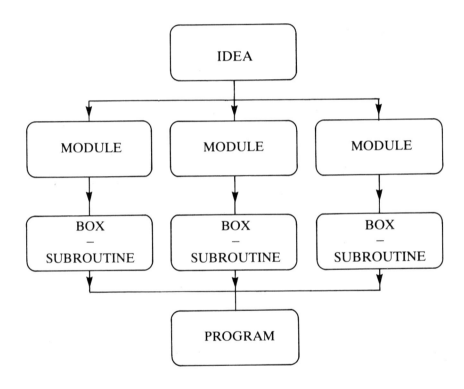

Figure 14.3

15 Stringing it Along

It's just possible—though I hope it's *not* the case—that you may be feeling that what I've done so far is all somewhat mathematical. I'm afraid that if you do think that, there's not much that can be done about it—computer programming *is* rather mathematical. By that I mean that it has to use numbers and relationships and has to involve fairly careful logical thinking.

The following direct command (direct so it doesn't need a line-number), I agree, may not appear to be mathematical.

PRINT "I am the BBC computer."

All the same, it really is mathematical in that:

1. Each character has to be converted to a number in the computer.
2. The numbers that result are grouped following certain rules— mathematical ones if you like.
3. The numbers move around in the micro following more such rules.
4. Mathematics, in a sense, is the process involved when the command is carried out, or when it is rejected because of an error.

All the same we don't need to think about all that, and in this chapter I'm going to tell you about *strings*—and we don't need to be too mathematical here.

WHAT IS A STRING?

As you've picked up long ago, a string is *any* set of characters. The characters in it can be alphabetical letters, numbers, punctuation marks, symbols—anything you can get from the keyboard. So "I am the BBC computer." is a string. So is "I have a 16K memory", and so are "3 × 6 = 18", "The year is/was 1982.", "What is your name?", "+, (− . / < 6a * Z", "24", and "□ □ □".

All these are what we call *string constants*—that means they don't change. String constants are enclosed by quote marks ("...") in writing and when communicating with the computer. (There is an interesting exception to the last point—string constants do not need quotes when held in DATA statements. I'll come back to that later.)

This quote mark rule means that *strings cannot contain quote marks*. Try this, for instance—and see why it can't work:

PRINT "I am the "BBC" computer."

The computer manages the first part—treating "I am the" as a string constant and printing it. Then it's told to PRINT BBC. It can do that only if BBC is a numeric variable with value, say, 20. Here it isn't, so we get the error report "No such variable".

If you need to use quotes in a string, the easiest thing to do is to use the apostrophe:

PRINT "I am the ' BBC ' computer." will be OK.

(There are complex ways to get double quotes into a string constant, but why bother?)

As well as having numeric constants (like 4) we have numeric variables (like A, where A could be *any* number). In the same way, again as you already know, we can have *string variables*. Here's one—N$ (say it "N string"). The dollar symbol after a variable name shows that this is a string variable. We've seen how to use this in earlier programs. It's like this:

```
10   INPUT "What is your name, Player 1", N$
20   PRINT ' ' "Thank-you, □"; N$; "."
30   INPUT "And what is yours, Player 2", M$
40   PRINT ' ' "Thank-you too, □"; M$; "."
50   CLS: PRINT "Right, □"; N$; "□ and □"; M$;
     "□ what you're going to have to do is □"          [and so on.]
```

Each time the program runs, the values of N$ and M$ will change—they are variables.

BBC BASIC has the following rule for "allowed" string variable names. A string variable name can be one or more characters. The first must be a letter; the others can be only letters and/or numbers. The length can be as much as you like (well, up to about 230 characters)—but as usual long names need care. Note that the letter(s) in a variable name can be upper case (capitals) or lower case (CAPS LOCK light off). I think the former are easier but some folk prefer lower case. This is because *a variable name should not contain a keyword* (like PRINT or TO).

As with numeric variable names:

1. You need a different name for each variable.
2. It's nice for a name to tell the reader something of its meaning (e.g. Name$), but:
3. Long names take up a lot of memory and can too easily be mis-typed.

BBC BASIC also has the same rules for string variables in PRINT statements as for numeric variables. Beware the semi-colon (;) though—you need to watch the spacing. See how I structured the string variable and constants in line 20 above, for instance.

STRING OPERATIONS

We can do all sorts of things with numeric constants and variables. We can add, subtract, raise to a power, multiply and divide. Well, we can add strings too, but the other operations do not have much meaning and can't be carried out as such.

The posh name for adding strings is *concatenation*. This means chaining together, and we use the + sign as with numbers. I've used the technique already, without comment— here's another example.

```
10   INPUT "What's your first name", FIRST$
20   INPUT ' "And your second", SECOND$
30   INPUT ' "Are you male (M) or female (F)", SEX$
40   CLS: PRINT "Thank-you, □";
50   IF SEX$ = "M" PRINT "Mr □"; ELSE PRINT "Ms □";
60   (LET) NAME$ = FIRST$ + "□" + SECOND$
70   PRINT NAME$; "."
```

The concatenation bit is in line 60. Got it?

In a PRINT statement we can have

either   PRINT X$; Y$

or   PRINT X$ + Y$.

Both have the same effect, but the latter (with +) is in fact a little smoother.

The above program also showed that we can use *logical operators* with strings, in decision statements—line 50. In fact we can use all the logical operators here: $<$, $<$ =, =, $>$ =, and $>$. Thus we can compare strings.

But what does that mean—how can one string be "greater" or "less" than a second? The ordering is in fact based on *ASCII codes*. Each character has a code, and what the micro does is to compare the strings character code by character code. (It has to do the same with the strings used in variable names and as that takes time it's another reason for using short names.)

Here are the main ASCII codes in summary. (I expect there will be a full list in the BBC *Manual*.)

Codes	Characters
0–32	(Special effects—see below)
33–47	Symbols
48–57	Numerals
58–64	Symbols
65–90	A–Z
91–96	Symbols
97–122	a–z
225–250	User-defined (Chapter 5)

Using these codes the micro can order strings in the same way as we can put names in alphabetical order. Thus:

ASMITH	<	BSMITH
SMITHA	<	SMITHB
SMITH	<	SMITHSON
SMITH1	<	SMITH2
12345	<	54321
12345	<	SMITH
SMITH	<	Smith
$MITH	<	SMITH

and so on. Please check that you agree with the above using the ASCII code list!

The next program uses all this to sort a list of twenty input strings into alpha (or ASCII) order. The input strings are called I$ (1), I$ (2) and so on up to I$ (20). This technique uses what's called a *string array*. You don't need to know more about it at the moment than this: before using an array tell the micro how big it is with a DIM (= dimension) statement. That's why I've put DIM I$ (20) in line 10—it tells the computer I'm going to have twenty strings, called I$ (1) . . . I$ (20).

The important thing here about this program is lines 70–100. Each time this section is reached it puts the two strings in question into the right order IF they need it (line 70). Spend a while working out how 80–100 sorts—it uses a valuable idea, that of a temporary store (here F$).

Program 17: Alphasort

```
10   DIM I$ (20)
20   FOR A = 1 TO 20
30   PRINT "Enter name □"; A; ": □": INPUT I$ (A)
40   NEXT A: A = 20: CLS
50   FOR C = 1 TO A − 1: D = 0
60   FOR E = 1 TO A − C
```

```
70   IF I$ (E + 1) > I$ (E) THEN 120
80   F$ = I$ (E)
90   I$ (E) = I$ (E + 1)
100  I$ (E + 1) = F$
110  D = 1
120  NEXT E
130  IF D = 0 THEN 150
140  NEXT C
150  FOR C = 1 TO A
160  PRINT I$ (C)
170  NEXT C
```

If you can't understand the rest of this program, don't worry—it's a very efficient one, but that makes it hard to grasp. Just concentrate on the string-handling in lines 70–100.

So, in a sense we *can* do "arithmetic" with strings. To summarize:

1.   We can add strings, like this

     LET A$ = N$ + "rules OK."

2.   We can compare strings, like this

     IF A$ < B$ OR C$ > = "TEST STRING" THEN LET E$ = F$

Here (again to repeat) a *string constant* is any set of keyboard characters (except " and ") between quote marks. And a string variable has the structure NAME$.

STRING FUNCTIONS

In Chapter 9 I discussed various numeric functions. Things like INT and SQR, these act on a numeric constant or variable to produce a number.

Thus INT (3.6) gives 3 and SQR (A) gives 4 if A = 2.

BASIC also has various string functions. We've already met one—LEN, which gives the number of characters in the string.

LEN ("Good morning!") = 13
and   LEN NAME$ = 5   if NAME$ = "Acorn"

LEN is a string function that produces a numeric result. Some string functions produce a string result. STRING$ is one I find useful; it's the nearest we've got (on any computer I know) to multiplying strings.

STRING$ (n, X$) produces a string of n copies of X$ added together. Thus LET A$ = STRING$ (2, "BYE") puts "BYEBYE" into A$, and LET BLANK$ = STRING$ (40, "□") makes BLANK$ into a line of forty spaces.

Here are some more string functions. I'll give a sample program using them after the notes!

ASC (". . .")   comes first. It gives the ASCII code (page 78) of the first character in the string in the brackets. PRINT ASC ("Arthur") gives 65 because 65 is the ASCII code of "A". Its opposite is:

CHR$ (n)   which gives the character whose ASCII code is n. The value of n should be between 0 and 255. Some ns give useful effects rather than characters. Thus PRINT CHR$ (12) will clear the screen, while CHR$ (8) has the effect of "backspace". Try—PRINT "I am the □"; CHR$ (34); "BBC"; CHR$ (34); "□ computer."

GET$ waits for a key press and then gives a string containing the character of the key. For instance,

    100   PRINT "Press 1, 2, 3 or 4."

    110   LET CHOICE$ = GET$

    120   IF CHOICE$ < "1" or CHOICE$ > "4" THEN GOTO 110

So it's a bit like INPUT but (a) doesn't give a prompt, (b) doesn't need (R), and (c) accepts only one character. There's a similar useful numeric function, GET, which is just the same except that it gives the ASCII value of the character entered.

*INKEY$*   (and its numeric counterpart INKEY) is almost the same as GET$, but this time it waits for a keypress only for a certain time. The time to wait is given as a number and works in hundredths of a second. Thus the previous example could be like this:

    100   PRESS "Press 1, 2, 3 or 4."

    110   LET CHOICE$ = INKEY$ (200)   [two seconds' wait]

    120   IF CHOICE$ = " " [i.e. nothing] THEN PRINT "Too late; my turn now."

    130   IF CHOICE$ < "1" OR CHOICE$ > "4" THEN PRINT "Mistake;

          my turn."

INSTR(A$, B$)   reports where in A$ the micro first finds B$. If the search is not successful the result is 0. Of course A$ must be longer than B$. Here's an example:

    100   INPUT "What's the capital of Argentina", ANS$

    110   IF ANS$ = "BUENOS AIRES" PRINT "Right!" ELSE

          IF INSTR(ANS$, "AIR") PRINT "Nearly—BUENOS AIRES" ELSE

          PRINT "No—it's BUENOS AIRES."

Note: Never put a space after INSTR.

LEFT$(BIG$, 3)   gives the first three (left-most three) characters of BIG$. Note there mustn't be a space after LEFT$. Thus:

    100   INPUT "Name", NAME$

    110   IF LEN(NAME$) > 6 PRINT "That's too long for me to remember.

          I'll just call you □"; LEFT$(NAME$, 6)

    120   NAME$ = LEFT$(NAME$, 6)

Line 120 won't cause problems, by the way, if LEN(NAME$) < = 6.

MID$(BIG$, 3, 2)   is rather similar—it gives the 3rd and 4th characters of BIG$: the middle starting at character 3 and taking 2 characters. Thus MID$("The BBC computer", 4, 3) = "BBC" and you can use things like

    IF MID$(A$, 9, 12) = LEFT$(B$, 4) THEN . . . or LET D$ = MID$(C$, 7, 5)

And then, of course, there's:

*RIGHT$*   which is just the reverse of LEFT$, counting from the righthand end of the string concerned instead of the left. So RIGHT$ ("The year is 1982.", 5) = "1982."

*STR$*   sounds strange, but is really very useful. It turns the number that follows it into a string. Then we can use it as a string instead of a number. So STR$(1982) = "1982". If, for instance, you want to print a long variable number (A) at the centre of line 2∅ in MODE 5, use this:

PRINT TAB (1∅ − LEN(STR$ (A)) / 2, 2∅);A

Can you work that out? It's a valuable trick. The opposite of STR$ is:

VAL   which turns a string into a number (if the string contents are numeric). Thus VAL ("1982") = 1982, but things like VAL ("BBC") give ∅. One major use is to check that a numeric input *is* a number and not a mistake. Like this:

1∅∅   INPUT "Give me a number." ' 'ANS$ [useful trick here!]

11∅   IF ANS$ < > "∅" AND VAL (ANS$) = ∅

PRINT "I said—a NUMBER!!": GOTO 1∅∅

Phew—there are quite a lot of string functions, aren't there? They all have major uses. Only practice can make you really familiar with them. Before I give you that practice, there's one more paragraph.

It's to note that, as with numbers, you can define your own string functions. The rules are the same (see Chapter 9):

1.   Give the function a name, including variable names concerned in brackets. Let's call it REP (A$).
2.   Define it somewhere in the program with DEF FN . . . = . . . Thus 1∅∅ DEF FNREP (A$) = STRING$ (N, A$)
3.   Call it when needed with PRINT FN name (variable), like this:

11∅   N = 5: X$ = "Hi!": PRINT FNREP (X$)

15∅   N = 3: PRINT FNREP (ANS$)

19∅   PRINT FNREP ("□ THE END □")

I doubt you'll have much need for defining your own string functions yet awhile, but that's enough to start you off when you do. Anyway, now I'll have a go at a program to use strings and string functions.

Program 18: Cat's cradle
(That's a joke about strings; we'll come to a real cat's cradle later . . .)

1∅   MODE 5: COLOUR 129: COLOUR ∅

2∅   PRINT CHR$ (12) + "Ready when you are.   . . ."

3∅   GO$ = INKEY$ (1∅∅)

It's known in the trade as a String-Handling Problem

```
40   IF GO$ = " " PRINT "Hurry up . . ."
50   GO$ = GET$
60   PRINT CHR$ (12) + "About time too"
70   A$ = "Cat's cradle"
80   A = 0: REPEAT: A = A + 1: PRINT TAB (RND (20 − LEN (A$) ) );
     LEFT$(A$, RND (LEN (A$) ) )
90   FOR B = 1 TO 150: NEXT: UNTIL A = 100
100  A = 0: REPEAT: A = A + 1: PRINT TAB (RND (20 − LEN (A$) ) );
     MID$ (A$, RND (LEN (A$) ), RND (LEN (A$) ) )
110  FOR B = 1 TO 100: NEXT: UNTIL A = 150
120  A = 0: REPEAT: A = A + 1: PRINT TAB (RND (20 − LEN (A$) ) );
     RIGHT$(A$, RND (LEN (A$) ) )
130  FOR B = 1 TO 50: NEXT: UNTIL A = 200
140  A = 0: REPEAT: A = A + 1: PROCOPEN (A$)
150  FOR B = 1 TO 200: NEXT: UNTIL A = 20
160  G = GET                          [wait for key press]
170  PRINT CHR$ (12) + CHR$ (10) + CHR$ (9) + "PHEW!!!"
180  PRINT ' ' "What's your name, bythe way?" ' ' '
190  INPUT N$: PRINT ' ' ' "Oh.": PAUSE$ = INKEY$ (100)
200  CLS: FOR A = 1 TO LEN (N$) * 2: PROCOPEN (N$): NEXT
210  G = GET
220  INPUT "Gimme your date of □ □ birth—like 050468" ' ' ' D$
230  CLS: D = VAL (D$)
240  FOR A = 1 TO 12
250  PRINT; A; " × "; D; " = "; A * D
260  NEXT
270  FOR WAIT = 1 TO 2000: NEXT: FOR A = 1 TO 10:
     PROCOPEN (D$): NEXT
280  FINAL$ = STRING$ (220 / (LEN (N$) + 1), N$ + "*")
290  CLS: PRINT FINAL$: G = GET: GOTO 10
300  DEF PROCOPEN (A$): LOCAL A
310  IF INT (LEN (A$) / 2) * 2 = LEN (A$) THEN A$ = A$ + "□"
320  FOR A = 1 TO LEN (A$) * 2 − 1 STEP 2
330  B$ = MID$(A$, LEN (A$) / 2 + 1 − A * 0.5, A):
     PRINT TAB (10 − LEN (B$) / 2); B$
340  NEXT: ENDPROC
```

To repeat line 170—"PHEW!!!". Did I imply that string-handling is not too mathematical? Oh, well, it's fun anyway. On purpose I'm not going to dissect Program 18.
That's up to you. There are some very useful routines in it—worth getting the hang of
them! Turn now to the projects to reinforce the ideas before you forget.

PROJECTS

1. Study Program A10 at the back of the book in the light of string-handling.
2. In MODE 5, as used in Program 18 (line 330) we can centre a set of characters in the line by PRINT TAB (10 − LEN (A$) / 2); A$. If the set of characters is a number, use PRINT TAB (10 − LEN (STR$ (A)) / 2); A. Lay out a screenful of titles etc. (like the title page of a book) using this routine in a procedure.
3. Get the Beeb's character set using a routine based on the following.

```
10   FOR A = 0 TO 255
20   PRINT A, CHR$ (A)
30   NEXT
```

   Beware the special effects . . . Record the values obtained if you do not have a table of BBC ASCII characters.
4. Use as many string operations and functions as you can (and need!) in a program to:
   (a) accept items of personal data about the user;
   (b) display the complete set of data neatly on screen.
5. Develop Program 15 to your own purposes.
6. Devise a pattern-generating program using STRING$.
7. Explore GET, GET$, INKEY and INKEY$ as ways of getting, checking and using keyboard input. Add VAL if you wish.
8. Devise a program with INSTR used usefully and meaningfully.

16 Swatting the Bugs

The story goes that in the very early days of electronic computing, four decades ago, incorrect operation was often traced to the activities of insects making their homes among the nice warm circuits. Alas, users of modern computers no longer have that excuse for program failures. Still, the use of the word "bug", to mean an unknown cause of software malfunction, remains. Here I would like to look very briefly at the process of "debugging", one of the last stages of program development.

In Chapter 12 I tried to describe a systematic approach to program development—the top-down modular approach. I have also noted that a program written as a series of subroutines is much easier to test. That's because you can test each subroutine on its own. In this chapter I shall discuss debugging approaches with a complete bugged program rather than a subroutine.

A BUGGED PROGRAM

The following program contains three major faults and several minor ones. I'd like you to enter it; as you do this, by all means look out for the faults. If you find any—feel proud, but do not correct them!

Program 19: Bugs (initial version)

```
10   VDU 23, 225, 0, 84, 57, 108, 254, 108, 57, 84
20   VDU 23, 226, 0, 5, 114, 90, 202, 138, 142, 0
30   VDU 23, 227, 0, 82, 36, 25, 62, 25, 36, 82
40   VDU 23, 228, 254, 130, 124, 74, 90, 66, 126, 0
50   MODE 5: COLOUR 128: COLOUR 1: CLS
60   FOR BUG = 1 TO 50
70   PRINT TAB (RND (20), RND (20) );
80   IF RND (4) = 1 THEN PRINT CHR$ (225): GOTO 120
90   IF RND (4) = 2 THEN PRINT CHR$ (226): GOTO 120
100  IF RND (4) = 3 THEN PRINT CHR$ (227): GOTO 120
110  IF RND (4) = 4 THEN PRINT CHR$ (228): GOTO 120
120  FOR A = 1 TO 130 PRINT TAB (A); "□ BUGS □": NEXT A
130  END
```

Entered? Don't RUN for a moment. First—can you see what this program is set up to do?

Lines 10–40 define four bugs (small creature type) and 50 sets up a MODE 5 screen. Then, lines 60–110, we print fifty random bugs at random screen sites. After that, 120–130, we display a diagonal title and stop.

Not a fantastic program—but does it work? Try it (key f0, don't forget). And you get one or two bugs—one error message, and perhaps one bug of the VDU 23 type. The error report tells us of a syntax error in line 120. Here's the line:

120   FOR A = 1 TO 130 PRINT TAB (A); "□BUGS□": NEXT A

I hope you can find, and correct the error yourself!

Key f0 again—and a great mess of a diagonal title, with a screen bug (insect) first if you're lucky. No error report this time—the program has run happily to the end. But it hasn't worked as planned.

For a start—no fifty insects. And if we'd got any we'd lose them with that diagonal title. Ah, wait a moment—that should be 30 in line 120, not 130—a typing error, with a profound effect. 30 lines in MODE 5, not 130! So line 120 should be:

120   FOR A = 1 TO 30: PRINT TAB (A); "□BUGS□": NEXT A

But it still doesn't work—the title doesn't start at the top of the screen, *and* it isn't a simple diagonal. The former is one of the three serious faults—can you explain it? Can you solve it? The latter is bad planning—there are thirty lines, but our title has six characters and there are only twenty character spaces in a line anyway.

To sort out both faults, *and* make the final cursor less annoying, several changes to 120 and 130 are needed. Here they are:

120   PRINT TAB (0, 0);: FOR A = 0 to 14: PRINT ' TAB (A);

      "□BUGS□": NEXT A

130   G = GET

Please try to understand these changes. The major fault is cured by the first statement in line 120, but can you see the value of the other changes?

But we still get no more than one "insect". Why's that? You've probably spotted the reason—major error number 2! The FOR in line 60 isn't matched by a NEXT anywhere. We *do* get an error report if there's a NEXT without a FOR—but the computer can't possibly spot the reverse problem. (Why not?) So we have to watch out for it all by ourselves!

Well, we need a NEXT BUG somewhere. And we need it before the title line, 120—so

115   NEXT BUG

OK? Simple!

RUN. OK? *Not* simple!—there's no change in the display. What's wrong? I guess you can see it—the GOTOs in lines 80–110 point at 120 rather than 115. We could change all those GOTO addresses, but let's be clever—delete 115, and put NEXT instead of GOTO 120 in each of those lines.

That gives us a much neater listing, less wasted memory, and, at last surely, a working program. RUN it.

Ah-ah. Still not fifty insects, are there? I tried to RUN this a couple of dozen times or more and the best I managed was seven. (Though some insects get "squashed" by the title.)

So for some reason, the loop does loop but never gets anywhere near its official two score and ten goes. We can check that readily enough, using a valuable little debugging trick. Add at the front end of 70—PRINT TAB (0, 1); BUG;. Now each time you run, you can see how far BUG gets; nowhere near 50, that's for sure. The printing out of carefully chosen variable values is an extremely useful aid to finding bugs in programs. Don't forget to remove the statements concerned when they're finished with, though.

TRACING

BBC BASIC has another useful debugging tool, called TRACE. TRACE ON causes the display of each line-number executed. TRACE OFF stops that display. You need TRACE OFF fairly close in a program to TRACE ON, because a screen full of line-numbers is rarely much help. What you *want* is to be able to trace the micro's path through no more than a dozen or so lines. You can then check on paper that the path is correct.

BBC BASIC's trace is very useful, when handled with care. It is however sometimes better to use your own TRACE statements in a few selected lines.

Say your program should follow through lines 100, 110, 170, 180, 120. Put PRINT 100 at the start of line 100, PRINT 110 at the start of 110 and so on—then you can see *exactly* what you need to examine. I reckon you won't need the full TRACE facility until you're into really big programs—but practise it and remember it when the time comes.

Anyway all that has given you time to work out what the bug is in *our* program . . . And its cause is tricky—but this is big fault number 3. Can you spot it? Figure 16.1 shows a flowchart of what I aimed at and Figure 16.2 shows a flowchart of what I actually have.

Can you see the subtle problem? The computer isn't choosing a number from 1 to 4 at random and then printing the corresponding insect. Is it? It's choosing a RND (4); if it's 1 it prints insect 1—if not, it chooses again. And so on. So the loop comes to a premature end whenever the micro's got to line 110 and chosen a number that isn't 4. Geddit?

How do we get over this problem? There are several ways. The one nearest the flowchart involves adding INSECT = RND (4) at the end of line 60 and changing RND (4) to INSECT in each of lines 80 –110. And—hooray—at last we've got somewhere! A nice display of random insects over the screen and the diagonal bugs title.

We've debugged BUGS and got it working as scheduled. We've cleared syntax and typing errors, reminded ourselves of correct loop structures, and seen that a flowchart *does* help program development. We've also emphasized the need for careful screen layout.

There are still problems left, and there are still ways we can structure the program better too (like putting 115 NEXT back in and clearing the NEXTs from the four preceding lines). Mainly the program's too fast—slow down the loop then. And it's a shame the title splats some of the insects so fast—a wait loop will solve that. And we could re-start after a while.

All that (and more) gives us this polished version. Check through with care . . .

Program 19: (final version)

```
10   VDU 23, 225, 0, 84, 57, 108, 254, 108, 57, 84

20   VDU 23, 226, 0, 5, 114, 90, 202, 138, 142, 0

30   VDU 23, 227, 0, 82, 36, 25, 62, 25, 36, 82

40   VDU 23, 228, 254, 130, 122, 74, 90, 66, 126, 0

50   MODE 5: COLOUR 128: COLOUR 1: CLS

55   REPEAT

60   FOR BUG = 1 TO 50: INSECT = RND (4)

70   FOR WAIT = 1 TO 1000: NEXT: PRINT TAB (RND (20) − 1,
     RND (30) − 1);: SOUND 1, −10, INSECT * 50, 2

80   IF INSECT = 1 PRINT CHR$ (225)

90   IF INSECT = 2 PRINT CHR$ (226)

100  IF INSECT = 3 PRINT CHR$ (227)

110  IF INSECT = 4 PRINT CHR$ (228)

115  NEXT: FOR WAIT = 1 TO 2000: NEXT
```

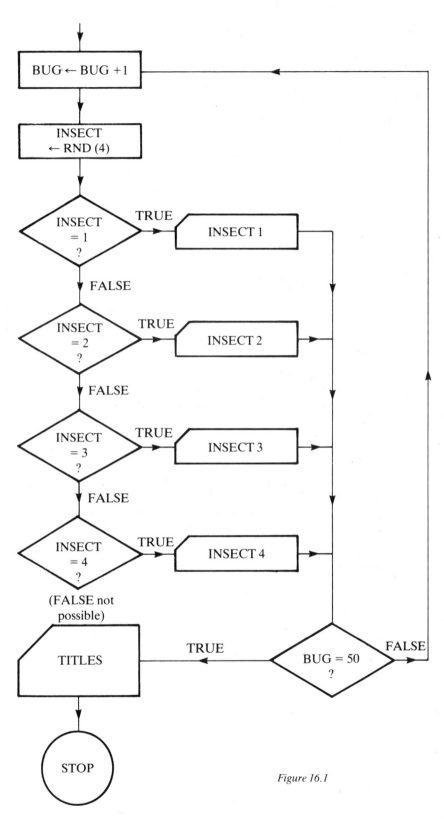

Figure 16.1

87

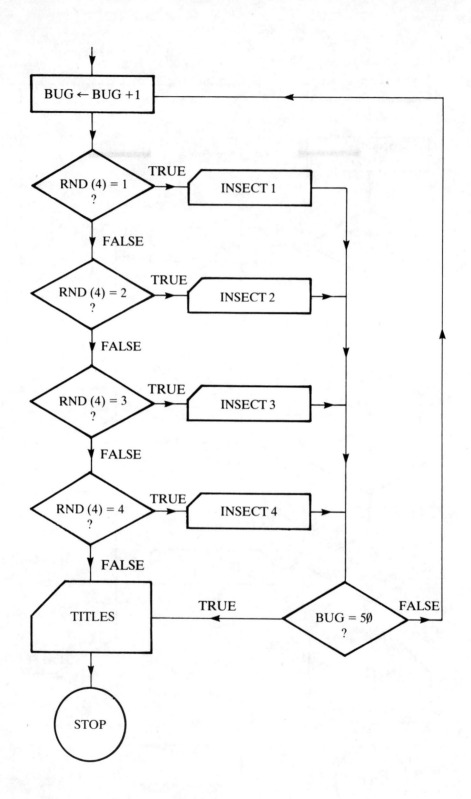

Figure 16.2

120   PRINT TAB (∅, ∅): FOR A = ∅ TO 14: PRINT ' TAB (A);

"□BUGS□": NEXT A

130   G = GET

140   UNTIL FALSE

SOME CLOSING TIPS

Other debugging tricks worth bearing in mind include these:

1. EDIT in a REM before a statement you don't want used for the time being. If you delete an offending statement, you may need to put it back later—and will you remember it? But beware of REMs in multi-statement lines—the REM will tell the computer to ignore everything after it.
2. Statements often worth REMoving in this way are ones with RND. It often helps to have a fixed value rather than a randomly varying one during testing. So think of changing, e.g.

   50   X = RND (10)   to   50   X = 5: REM X = RND (10)

   if you have RND problems.
3. Use REPORT if a program with ON ERROR doesn't work properly. REPORT will then display the last error message (but not in as much detail as usual). If there wasn't an error to report, you get a message from Acorn. Many will think there's an error in that message!

But the best way to reduce the trials of debugging is not to have bugs in the first place. Well, none of us is perfect—we all make *some* programming mistakes! All the same, the modular, top-down, flowchart-based approach I've discussed earlier is a great help to bug-prevention. And if your program's in modules, you'll find it *much* easier to sort out if it does go wrong.

17 A Sound Time

The main topic I'd like to introduce in this chapter is the programming of the BBC's sophisticated sound generation system. That system *is* sophisticated and I've no intention of taking it very far—a full analysis would require a book half the length of this.

As you know, the Beeb has its own internal speaker, a small but quite good one under the left-hand side of the cover. It is not difficult to take the signal instead to a more powerful speaker (or two), with or without an amplifier. This does, however, require your working inside the case, and that could invalidate the guarantee. People rarely try to feed sound to the TV speaker, for technical reasons; however it can be done and ought to be done.

First allow me to set out a little background physics.

SOUND THEORY

Think of a single note produced by vibration in some musical instrument or other source. We describe it in terms of five factors:

1. *Loudness*—is it strong or faint? The posh term for loudness is *amplitude*. The vibrations are more violent in the case of a loud sound (high amplitude) than a soft one.
2. *Pitch*—is it low or high? Sounds from the left-hand keys of a piano (or a man's throat) are lower pitched than those from the right (or a female voice). Pitch relates to what scientists call the *frequency* of vibration—to obtain a low pitch there are fewer vibrations in a second.
3. *Quality* (or *timbre*)—is the sound pure or rough? The difference between the sounds of, say, a trumpet and a guitar playing the same note is a difference in quality. What's really happening is that there are different tones, of different amplitudes and frequencies, in each sound.
4. *Attack*—how does the sound start, continue and stop? You may have heard tapes of a piano played backwards—the result is not like a piano at all because the attack is reversed.
5. *Duration*—how long does the sound last?

BEEB SOUND

As I said, the sound facility of the BBC micro is very sophisticated. Uniquely among micros, it allows the user to program all five of the above factors of a sound. (Most micros, if they have sound at all, allow control only of pitch (frequency) and duration.)

Partly this is because the Beeb has three-channel sound, allowing three separately programmed notes to be "played" together—giving chords as well as good control over quality. (There is in fact a fourth sound channel—for special effects—which I'll deal with separately.)

To control all these factors from instant to instant gives the Beeb the potential of a fairly good synthesizer. However it is *not* a synthesizer, so you have to do a lot of work to get anything like real music. Don't be ambitious, at first anyway—stick to simple beeps and warbles, simple sequences of notes and sounds. Don't accept the challenge (found in the manual of another micro) to program the whole movement of a symphony—it would be quicker to learn to play the piano!

The BBC micro has two keywords in this context—ENVELOPE, which controls attack, and SOUND which causes the speaker to operate. I'll start with the latter. Work through these examples and notes.

1. The SOUND command/statement has this structure (or syntax). Spaces are optional throughout.

    SOUND   C, V, F, D

    Here   C is channel: 1, 2 or 3 (or $\emptyset$ for special effects)
    V is volume: -15 (loud) to -1 (very soft) (or 1–4 for envelopes)
    F is frequency: $\emptyset$ (low) to 255 (high)
    D is duration: $\emptyset$ (short) to 254 (12½ seconds)

    Explore these effects by giving direct SOUND commands (changing them with EDIT). For the time being keep C = 1. Here are some examples:

SOUND 1, -15, 1, $\emptyset$	[click]
SOUND 1, -15, 1, 1$\emptyset$	[half-second low tone]
SOUND 1, $-1\emptyset$, 1, 1$\emptyset$	[a quieter one]
SOUND 1, $-1\emptyset$, 1$\emptyset\emptyset$, 1$\emptyset$	[a higher one]
SOUND 1, -15, 25$\emptyset$, 1$\emptyset\emptyset$	[a long, loud squeak]

2. Frequency (F) control involves the third of the four SOUND variables. Its value can be between $\emptyset$ (just below middle C) to 255 (just over five octaves higher). Other values, plus or minus, are allowed—but they have the same effect as ones in the range.

    Generally speaking, each step between 1 and 255 corresponds to a quarter of a semi-tone, with middle C (roughly) at 5, and the other Cs at 53, 1$\emptyset$1, 149, 197 and 245. (There are twelve semi-tones in an octave.) The SOUND control accepts decimal fraction values of F, but my poor ear can't detect any difference from the corresponding INTegral ones. Thus this:

    FOR A = 1 TO 2$\emptyset$: SOUND 1, -15, 157, 1$\emptyset$:
    SOUND 1, -15, 156.999, 1$\emptyset$: NEXT

    sounds the same as having just 156 in the second sound.

3. Duration is controlled by D, the fourth variable of SOUND. Ranging from 1 to 254, the value gives the time in twentieths of a second. That seems more accurate than the frequency control. (Or is my piano more out of tune than my watch?) D = $\emptyset$ gives a little click (whatever the frequency setting). D = 255 on the other hand gives a sound for ever—until you ESCAPE or BREAK anyway.

    According to Acorn, an infinite-duration sound will also stop if you send another SOUND signal for processing. This may not always be so—so avoid 255 durations unless you want to drive the neighbours potty. Use a REPEAT: SOUND . . .: UNTIL loop instead.

A ONE-CHANNEL PROGRAM

Because each note must be specified individually, programming tunes can be tedious. No doubt synthesizer software for the Beeb will soon appear—but meanwhile, if you want tunes you'll have to put up with the tedium.

Here's the best way I've found to go about it:

1. Choose a short, easy tune that you know!

2. Pick it out on a piano and write down the order of notes. You'll be able to remember the durations and rests.
3. Set *KEY Ø "RUN ¦ M"
        *KEY 1 "SOUND 1, −15,"
        *KEY 2 "SOUND 1, Ø, Ø,"
        *KEY 10 "OLD ¦ M LIST ¦ M"
        AUTO
4. Then program:
    For each note press f1 and enter the F-value (see Figure 17.1) and duration (say 10 per crotchet).
    For each rest press f2 and enter the duration.
5. ESCAPE, f1Ø to check, fØ to RUN—and then get polishing.

A	B♭	B	C	C♯	D	E♭	E	F	F♯	G	G♯
	Ø	1	5	9	13	17	21	25	29	33	37
41	45	49	53	57	61	65	69	73	77	81	85
89	93	97	1Ø1	1Ø5	1Ø9	113	117	121	125	129	133
137	141	145	149	153	157	161	165	169	173	177	181
185	189	193	197	2Ø1	2Ø5	2Ø9	213	217	221	225	229
233	237	241	245	249	253						

□ middle C

Figure 17.1

I did all that, and also used another trick to save time, pre-setting crotchet and quaver durations first, to get this program:

Program 20: Call the RSPCA

```
1Ø   C = 1Ø: Q = 5                    [durations]
2Ø   FOR A = 1 TO 2
3Ø   SOUND 1, −15, 21, C              [note]
4Ø   SOUND 1, −15, 13, C
5Ø   SOUND 1, −15, 5, C
6Ø   SOUND 1, Ø, Ø, C                 [rest]
7Ø   NEXT A
8Ø   FOR A = 1 TO 3
9Ø   SOUND 1, −15, 33, C
1ØØ  SOUND 1, −15, 53, C
11Ø  SOUND 1, −15, 49, Q
12Ø  SOUND 1, −15, 41, Q
13Ø  SOUND 1, −15, 49, Q
14Ø  SOUND 1, −15, 53, C + Q
15Ø  SOUND 1, −15, 33, C
16Ø  SOUND 1, Ø, Ø, Q
17Ø  NEXT A
```

```
18Ø    SOUND 1, −15, 25, Q
19Ø    SOUND 1, −15, 21, C
2ØØ    SOUND 1, −15, 13, C
21Ø    SOUND 1, −15, 5, C
```

Did you notice something interesting when running that (apart from the virtuosity of the music)? If not, RUN again and watch the line below RUN on the screen. As soon as the program got to line 16Ø for the last time, the READY prompt appeared.

A major feature of BBC sound is that SOUND statements can queue up in a special section of memory to be processed in turn while the micro gets on with other things. And *that* gives us the possibility of . . .

MULTI-CHANNEL SOUND

You have (I hope) been fairly good at sticking to channel 1 so far. Now try this:

```
1Ø    SOUND 1, −15, 41, 2ØØ       [A]
2Ø    SOUND 1, −15, 53, 2ØØ       [C]
3Ø    SOUND 1, −15, 19, 2ØØ       [E]
4Ø    GOTO 1Ø                     [as long as you can stand it]
```

You *should* hear a three-note chord (the chord of A major they call it) but, alas, you're now pushing this non-synthesizer a bit hard, and you'll get less than hi-fi. It's not a *bad* chord, but there are strange interference effects and buzzes—the result of imperfect electronics and speaker in particular.

All the same, you now have the basis for simple multi-channel "music". Experiment on the following lines.

Program 21: Random chords

```
1Ø     A = Ø: REPEAT: A = A + 1Ø
2Ø     SOUND 1, −1Ø, A, 5Ø
3Ø     SOUND 1, −15, A*A, 2Ø
4Ø     SOUND 1, Ø, Ø, 3Ø
5Ø     SOUND 2, −15, A*3, 4Ø
6Ø     SOUND 2, −1Ø, A/2, 1Ø
7Ø     SOUND 2, Ø, Ø, 6Ø
8Ø     SOUND 3, −15, A+2Ø, 2Ø
9Ø     SOUND 3, −15, 3ØØ/A, 3Ø
1ØØ    SOUND 3, Ø, Ø, 4Ø
11Ø    UNTIL A = 1ØØ
```

Use TRACE ON while playing with these ideas; introduce RND into your statements as well as putting loudness and duration under variable control.

Or you can try looping, like this, as part of your repertoire.

```
1Ø    FOR A = Ø TO 255
2Ø    SOUND 1, −15, A, .1
3Ø    NEXT
```

But ENVELOPE does it better . . .

```
10  ENVELOPE 4, 2, −1, 10, 5, 50, 50, 50, 5, 0, 0, 1, 126, 127
20  SOUND 1, 4, 0, 10
30  SOUND 2, 4, 100, 20
40  SOUND 3, 4, 200, 30
50  GOTO 10
```

That shows the power of ENVELOPE, which controls sounds by shaping them to a pattern of frequency and loudness. Partly that is the *attack* I mentioned before. But you can believe that, with 14 control variables, ENVELOPE is a complex beast to handle. I can't say much more about it here, but you will find plenty on it in magazine articles and more advanced books.

Up to four ENVELOPES can be in action at the same time. SOUND statements refer to them by having 1–4 as the value of V. I used envelope 4 in the above example. That number is also the first, A, of the 14 envelope variables. The others, B–N in brief, control

B	speed at which one goes through the envelope's four parts
C–E	rate of frequency change in parts 1, 2 and 3
F–H	speed at which one passes through each part
I–L	rate of volume change in parts 1, 2, 3 and 4
M–N	volume levels at ends of parts 1 and 2

Some of these variables are shown in Figure 17.2.

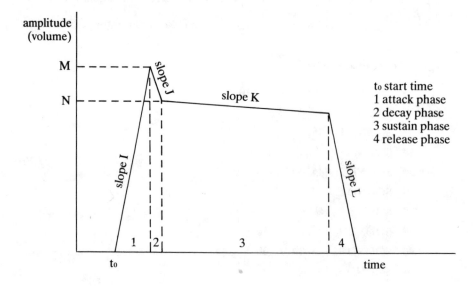

Figure 17.2

94

CHANNEL 0

You may have thought we've had special effects already with the ENVELOPE concept. However ENVELOPE + SOUND still gives us only pure notes (fairly pure anyway). Channel 0, called special effects sound, produces *noise*. Noise is a mixture of pure notes like the sound of a radio or TV when there's no station at that setting, or the sound you make called "shh". We access channel 0 with:

    SOUND 0, V, effect, D   [V—volume; D—duration]

The value of "effect" can be between 0 and 7:

0	high frequency buzz
1	medium frequency buzz
2	low frequency buzz
3	buzz of frequency depending on that in channel 1
4–7	"shh" noises similarly

Experiment with SOUND 0, −15, effect, 10. Add such lines to the little envelope program above and see how channel 1 statements affect them.

    Well. I *did* say that Beeb sound needs a book of its own. It's a quite fascinating topic. You're best advised to start into it not with music, but by designing suitable sounds to go with different parts of your programs. but don't overdo it—you'll lose all your friends if you're not careful!

    No projects this time; I think I've given you plenty to work with . . .

18 Ragbag

This is the last Utilities chapter in the book, the last one dealing with various facilities not strictly to do with programming as such. But I'm not being strict, and shall here look at some aspects of BBC BASIC not dealt with elsewhere.

In particular I shall note three important areas for the advanced programmer that an introductory book like this should not attempt to touch. These are: interfacing the computer with other equipment; dealing with what are called files; and programming in so-called machine code.

TRUE UTILITIES

First let's look at two commands of use when working on lengthy programs.

DELETE (the command, not the key next to COPY) is used to remove whole chunks of a program from memory. To remove the odd line is easy—you just type the line-number and (R). However, you may have the need to remove a set of dozens of lines. This may happen if you'd put the set starting at 3000, then transferred it to 4000 (using EDIT) for some reason. To remove the surplus set from 3000 would be tedious if you had to use line-number + (R). So we have DELETE.

The structure of this command is DELETE n1, n2. Here n1 is the first line number of the surplus block and n2 is the last. When you press (R) and then LIST, you'll find that all lines between n1 and n2 inclusive have gone. Gone for ever, too—you can't get them back with OLD . . .

The command structure is thus a bit like LIST n1, n2, then. However, you cannot use DELETE, n2 or DELETE n1, to remove the last or first parts of a program. This is a pity. To remove everything up to, say, 999, use DELETE 0, 999 or DELETE n1, 999 (n1 being the first line in the program). To remove everything after, say, 999, use DELETE 1000, 32767 (the highest line-number allowed), or DELETE 1000, n2 (n2 being the last line in the program). The computer accepts DEL. for DELETE.

RENUMBER (REN.) is quite useful but not very flexible. There are three forms:

RENUMBER (R) will give a program starting 10, 20, 30, etc.
RENUMBER n1 (R) will give n1, n1 + 10, n1 + 20, etc.
RENUMBER n1, n2 (R) gives n1, n1 + n2, n1 + 2 × n2, etc.

The addresses of all GOTO and GOSUB statements will be changed to suit the new numbers.

As you know, I like to set out long programs with blocks in different positions in memory (100, 500, 1000 and so on). It is not possible, however, to renumber *part* of a program, so we still need planning. Do not, therefore, get used to REN. as a way of rescuing yourself from a mess!

DATA

The facility to "read" data stored in a program exists in most BASICs. A hangover from the early days of computing, it is, in my view, not often very useful now. However, there are occasions when it is of real value. Those occasions concern situations where a program has to process different chunks of data in a certain sequence and those chunks do not change.

We could have a letter game program, for instance, in which the player has to guess, one by one, a set of letters. Here are two approaches (both very crude demonstrations):

1. Using INPUT—a second player enters each letter in secret first:

    10 REPEAT: INPUT "Player 2, what is letter to guess", GUESS$

    20 CLS

    30 INPUT "Player 1, what is the letter", TRY$

    40 IF TRY$ = GUESS$ PRINT "Right" ELSE PRINT "Wrong"

    50 G = GET: CLS: UNTIL FALSE   [re-start]

    This approach gives maximum flexibility.
2. Using an array (we met arrays briefly in Chapter 15, and I'm going to deal with them fully soon):

    10 DIM GUESS$ (20)

    20 (LET) GUESS$ (1) = "F"

    30 (LET) GUESS$ (2) = "X"

    40 etc.

    300 FOR GO = 1 TO 20

    310 CLS: INPUT "What is the letter", TRY$

    320 IF TRY$ = GUESS$ (GO) PRINT "Right" ELSE PRINT "Wrong"

    330 G = GET: NEXT GO

    340 STOP   [no re-start]

This gives less flexibility, but is easier on Player 2 even if tedious to program. (Still, EDIT makes the assignments fairly easy.) READ . . . DATA offers just as little flexibility as (2), but is not so tedious to program. Here's our routine now:

    10 REPEAT: ON ERROR GOTO 100

    20 READ GUESS$: CLS

    30 INPUT "What is the letter", TRY$

    40 IF TRY$ = GUESS$ PRINT [and so on]

    50 UNTIL FALSE

    60 DATA "F", "X", "D" [etc.]

    100 CLS: PRINT "Game over"

    110 STOP   [no re-start]

This uses two new keywords. *READ* GUESS$ (line 10) tells the computer to fetch the first unused item from the *DATA* list (line 60) and call it GUESS$.

We can imagine there's a sort of pointer attached to the DATA list. Each time READ fetches an item from the list the pointer moves on one place. In our case, if the list carries twenty items (separated by commas, note), the program can use READ twenty times, with different values of GUESS$ each time.

What happens then? The DATA list pointer has come to the end, so the next READ will have nothing to fetch. That will lead to the error report "Out of DATA" (number 42)—I've trapped this with the ON ERROR GOTO 100 in the first line. (See Chapter 9.)

If we want a re-start we can use a third keyword—RESTORE. This tells the computer to "restore" the pointer to the start of the list. To stick with our letter game I could do this, therefore:

10   REPEAT: ON ERROR RESTORE

and cut out lines 100 and 110. Then the game would go on for ever (until ESCAPE), with the same set of letters coming up again and again in the same sequence.

However we can add a degree of flexibility by using RESTORE n, where n is a line-number. Each time RESTORE n is met, the pointer will move to n and the next READ will dig up the first DATA item listed there.

Now, then, we can have the 26 possible letters in 26 separate DATA statements, and access them at random with a RESTORE (random n to n + 26) statement. That gives us this version of the game:

Program 22: Letter guess

```
10   MODE 5
20   REPEAT: RESTORE (99 + RND (26) )
30   READ GUESS$: CLS
40   REPEAT: INPUT ' "What letter", TRY$
50   PRINT TAB (6): IF TRY$ < GUESS$ PRINT "Too low!" ELSE
     IF TRY$ > GUESS$ PRINT "Too high!"
60   UNTIL TRY$ = GUESS$
70   PRINT ' ' ' "That's it!!": FOR WAIT = 1 TO 7000: NEXT
80   UNTIL FALSE                [repeat for ever]
100  DATA A                     [space not needed]
101  DATA B
102  DATA C [and so on]
```

Most uses of READ . . . DATA you may meet have little, if any, advantage over either INPUT or (LET). Using it with the RESTORE n facility makes it powerful in a number of "serious" games situations.

A couple more little points about READ . . . DATA. First note lines 100 onwards in Program 22: there is no need to distinguish between strings and numeric data—we don't need quote marks in the former case. This unique BBC feature is very helpful, even if theoretically dangerous. (You *can* put string DATA in quotes if you like—the Beeb doesn't mind—and you *must* do so if the string in question starts with one or more spaces or contains a comma.)

READ is fairly flexible. You can follow it with one or more variable labels (string or numeric—but they must match the DATA items), separated by commas as with INPUT.

Here are fragments of a possible record collection program.

```
1000   REM ** SEARCH ROUTINE **
1010   INPUT "What group", GROUP$: PROCSPACE
1020   FOR A = 1 TO 50               [if 50 records]
1030   READ RECORD$
```

```
1040  IF LEFT$(RECORD$, 20) = GROUP$ THEN PRINT ' GROUP$ '
      TAB (3);MID$(RECORD$, 21, 20) ' TAB (5); RIGHT$(RECORD$, 20)
1050  NEXT A
```

This implies that each record is held in data as a sixty-character string in three parts (group, title, things like label and date). Each part *must* contain twenty characters so you would need to fill up with blanks if required (PROC SPACE). Each data statement would have the form

DATA GROUP [15 spaces]   DISC TITLE [10 spaces]   LABEL + DATE [10 spaces]

This is fairly unwieldy, though it would work. It would be better to use arrays (Chapter 20) in practice. Or even FILES.

FILE-HANDLING

I have no intention of saying much about this rather advanced aspect of BBC BASIC here.

A *file* is any collection of data held in cassette (or otherwise) and able to be called upon by the process unit of a computer. So BASIC programs saved on cassette are really files—we access them using LOAD or CHAIN.

BBC file-handling is designed for the disc system. Most users will stick with cassettes, at least for the time being—they are far cheaper, although much slower.

1. Opening a file—this must be done before a file is used. The structure (command or program line) is

    F = OPENOUT "name"

    Here F can be any numeric variable and "name" any string. For instance

    1000 INPUT "File-name", F$

    1010 F = OPENOUT F$

2. Writing to a file—this means sending data. The structure is very like that of a mixed PRINT statement (except only comma separators are valid):

    1020 PRINT # F, data, string, "EXAMPLE"

    The hash symbol # (on the 3 key) tells the computer which file to write to (but in cassette filing you can write to only one at a time).
3. Closing a file—this must be done when no more data is to be sent.

    1030 CLOSE # F

4. Reading from a file—this means recapturing data. First the file must be re-opened—this time, as the file already exists, by using OPENIN rather than OPENOUT. Then we use INPUT for the actual reading action:

    2000 F = OPENIN "name"

    (a different variable may be used—but you *must* of course call the right name!)

    2010 INPUT # F, number, name, EXAMPLE$

    2020 CLOSE # F

5. Other related keywords are

    BPUT #   write a single byte to the file
    BGET #   read a single byte from the file
    IF EOF # ... check for the End Of the File

MACHINE-CODING

Like most micros, the Beeb can accept instructions in low-level code rather than high-level BASIC form. It has what is called an *assembler* facility for this purpose. Such work is fairly advanced and I shall say little about it here—however there are major advantages of assembler programming. In particular such routines work dozens of times faster than the corresponding BASIC ones.

Machine code sections of BASIC programs must open with "["(next to ⑥, coming out as ← in MODE 7). They must close with "]" (next to (R), → in MODE 7).

Relevant keywords are:

DIM section name N
P% = section name — reserve N bytes of memory for the section
CALL section name   [tells the section to execute]

INTERFACING

This concerns using the micro to capture information from outside devices and/or to control outside devices. Examples of the two types are photocells and electronic thermometers, and lamps and motors.

You can use the cassette control in the standard Beeb to some extent for controlling other devices. Otherwise you need to have suitable interfaces connected to your micro; Model B has some. The ADVAL command is used with Model B interfacing to convert the analog signal of say, a photocell, to the digital data form the micro needs.

Uses of interfacing include:

controlling tape-slide equipment from an interactive program
burglar alarms
flashing light displays
central heating control.

19 A Graphic Description

And now we come to the last major untouched area of BBC BASIC programming—graphics. This includes all aspects of "drawing" and "painting" as applied to a colour microcomputer—the generation of points, lines and shapes, and the blocking in of areas of solid colour.

As is the case with BBC sound programming the graphics facility is very sophisticated and therefore not always straightforward.

MODES

Of course you know that the Beeb has a number of different "modes" of operation. When you switch it on, you get MODE 7, the teletext mode. (This is the one you would use if you link your micro to Prestel.)

Throughout this book so far, we have concentrated on MODE 5 (the Model A's graphics mode) or MODE 7. Here is a full list of the eight modes.

MODE	Text	Zones	Colours	Graphics	Memory /K
7	25 × 40	4	b/w	No	1
6	25 × 40	4	2	No	8
5	32 × 20	2	4	160 × 256	10
4	32 × 40	4	2	320 × 256	10
3	32 × 80	8	2	No	16
2	32 × 20	2	16	160 × 256	20
1	32 × 40	4	4	640 × 256	20
0	32 × 80	8	2	640 × 256	20

The "text" column shows the number of lines of text and the number of characters allowed in each line. For text we measure (with TAB) from position (0, 0) at top left of the screen. Print zones (Chapter 5) contain ten character positions each, hence the data in the third column.

In the "colours" column I show the number of on-screen colours allowed at any time (see Chapter 7). The "graphics" data give the number of horizontal and vertical points you can plot at. You can't plot in MODES 3, 6 or 7 (though in the first two, as in all the graphics modes, you can use your own VDU 23 characters—Chapter 5 again). There are techniques—very good ones—for getting the colours in MODE 7 strings, but the techniques are beyond this book.

The last column tells you how much memory the micro reserves for its own needs as soon as you enter a given mode. The more complex a display can be, the more memory is reserved. The Model A Beeb has only 16K memory available for this and your programs so you can't get MODES 3–0 with it.

The unit of memory size is the "K". This stands for 1024 of the memory units called *bytes*. (A byte is eight bits if you know about such things.) The programs in this book don't go over 2K, so you can run them in any available mode if you want. But clearly you'd be in trouble if you wanted to run a 7K program in Model A's MODE 5—and you'd get a cheerful error report.

You call the mode you want, as you know, by MODE X. This can be done as a direct command or within a program (except in a procedure). MODE such and such clears the screen, by the way. All the same I suggest you always use CLS after it to remind you to think about layout. The statement also gives you a black screen unless background colour has been defined.

THE DRAW COMMAND

This instructs the computer to draw a line—it is a graphics command so does not work in MODES 3, 6 or 7. What it does is to draw a line from some previous point to the one whose coordinates you specify after the keyword.

We need a bit of background knowledge to get the hang of the coordinates concept. Look at Figure 19.1. The screen is always (whatever the mode) pictured in the computer as comprising 1024 lines (y-values) each of 1280 points (x-values). This is a bit imaginary as no BBC mode currently available can actually access such small points, and no TV set could show them. All the same, Acorn are (among other things) planning for the future.

Anyway, like the simple graphs you've probably drawn at school, we have a co-ordinate system here, based on an origin O ($x = 0, y = 0$) at the bottom left corner of the graphics area.

Point A in the sketch below is 100 steps across and 300 steps up. Its x, y coordinates are (100, 300) and if we use DRAW 100, 300 we should get a line to it. As long as we're in a graphics mode. Where's the line from? If the micro isn't told otherwise, it'll draw the line to A from the origin. Try it.

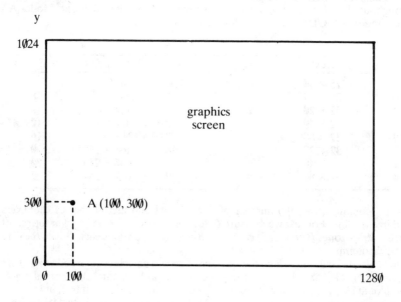

Figure 19.1

The next program gives you the basis for using DRAW in each mode. It's written for Model A; Model B users should change 4 in line 10 to 0. I'll explain the program after the listing.

Program 23: Your move

```
10   FOR M = 4 TO 7                          [Model A]
20   MODE M: COLOUR 2
30   PROCDRAW
40   NEXT
50   STOP
60   DEF PROCDRAW
70   CLS: VDU 5
80   DRAW 100, 300
90   PRINT "A"
100  MOVE 100, 300
110  DRAW 700, 700
120  PRINT "B";
130  DRAW 10, 10
140  PRINT "C"
150  INPUT "X (< 1000), Y (< 1000)", X, Y
160  MOVE X, Y: PRINT "Mode □"; M
170  G = GET
180  ENDPROC
```

Notes: VDU 5 (line 70) allows you to mix print (text) and graphics fully. It hides the cursor in graphics modes and lets you print literally anywhere (as in lines 160–170).

DRAW 100, 300 (line 80) gives a line from 0, 0 to that point, A. We then (line 90) print "A" starting at that point.

MOVE 100, 300 (line 100) is to get us back to point A after doing the printing. See the difference at point B as a result of the different structure of line 120: PRINT rules are still followed!

Play around with this program. Observe with care the effects of different PRINT positions (as in line 140 above) and the effects of moving or drawing or printing outside the 1280 × 1024 screen. Become aware of the features of the different graphics modes you have available.

Use the next program in the same kind of way. This also introduces the technique of colour control in graphics modes.

Program 24: A real cat's cradle?

```
10   MODE 5: ON ERROR GOTO 120
20   VDU 19, 0, 10, 0, 0, 0                  [flashing green background]
30   VDU 19, 1, 11, 0, 0, 0                  [flashing yellow foreground]
40   CLS: VDU 5
50   line = 0
60   REPEAT: line = line + 1
70   X1 = RND (1280): X2 = RND (1280)
80   Y1 = RND (1024): Y2 = RND (1024)
90   MOVE X1, Y1: DRAW X2, Y2
100  PRINT line
```

110	UNTIL FALSE	
120	VDU 19, 0, 1, 0, 0, 0	[red background]
130	VDU 19, 0, 0, 0, 0, 0	[black foreground]
140	REPEAT: UNTIL FALSE	

Notes: First the VDU 19 command, the way to get non-standard colours in graphics modes. Non-standard? Well, I guess I'd first best say what the *standard* colours are . . .

MODES 0, 3, 4 and 6 may be called two-colour graphics modes—only two colours can be on screen at once. These bear the "logical" colour numbers 0 and 1 and normally give black background and white foreground. MODES 1 and 5 allow four colours whose standard "logical" numbers and values are:

0 Black
1 Red
2 Yellow
3 White

You met these values in Chapter 7, with the COLOUR statement.

MODE 2 is an eight-colour mode (or sixteen, depending on your point of view):

0	Black	8	Flashing black/white
1	Red	9	Flashing red/cyan
2	Green	10	Flashing green/magenta
3	Yellow	11	Flashing yellow/blue
4	Blue	12	Flashing blue/yellow
5	Magenta	13	Flashing magenta/green
6	Cyan	14	Flashing cyan/red
7	White	15	Flashing white/black

VDU 19 allows you to change a "logical" colour in any graphics mode to one of those in the above list. Its structure is VDU 19, logical colour, required colour, 0, 0, 0.

Lines 20 and 30 above use this. They make foreground and background flash—and that flashing will go on after the program's stopped. To avoid that problem I've trapped the use of ESCAPE, in line 10—when you want to stop the program with ESCAPE, the VDU 19 calls lines 120 and 130 into action. They stop the flashing and fix the picture for quiet examination.

Line 140, by the way, prevents the "finished" cursor from appearing. However, the error trap means that only BREAK will get you out! (This is called "disabling" the ESCAPE key—I have already noted how to disable BREAK.)

THE PLOT COMMAND

PLOT is the most versatile graphics command. MOVE and DRAW are in fact special names for the two most common of its 56 variations. (There will be more variations in later versions of the Beeb.) The structure is

PLOT V, X, Y

where V is the variation number and X and Y are as before. The allowed values of V provide the following facilities. I'll explain the numbers in brackets in a moment.

Move to X, Y
—measured from (0, 0) (4) or from the previous point (0);
—without drawing (0), drawing a continuous line (0), drawing a dotted line (16), leaving out the last point in the line (8);
—marking the point X, Y with a dot (64) or not (0);
—filling the triangle between X, Y and the two previous points (80) or not (0);
—using foreground colour (1), the inverse of the foreground colour (2), the background colour (3) or no colour (0).

Any plot action you want must be described by choosing one statement from each of the above five lines. Then you get that action by making the value of V the sum of the corresponding numbers. Like this . . .

Program 25: Morning Cloud

1. You are now at 200, 700, having last been at 100, 100. Get there with:

10	MODE 4: VDU 5	
20	VDU 19, 0, 3, 0, 0, 0	[yellow background]
30	VDU 19, 1, 1, 0, 0, 0	[red foreground]
40	CLG	[truly clear screen]
50	MOVE 100, 100	
60	MOVE 200, 700	
200	REPEAT: UNTIL FALSE	[keep out cursor]

2. To plot a triangle between those two points and 1000, 100:

Measuring from origin	4
Without drawing	0
Without dotting	0
Fill triangle	80
In inverse colour (cyan)	2
	86 = V

    70   PLOT 86, 1000, 100   [pretty!]

3. To draw a dotted vertical from the second point:

Measure from origin	4
Draw dotted line complete	16
No extra dot	0
No triangle	0
Background colour	3
	23 = V

    80   MOVE 200, 700

    90   PLOT 23, 200, 100

4. Take that to edge of screen:

Measure from last point	0
Draw dotted line complete	16
No extra dot or triangle	0
Foreground colour	1
	17 = V

    100   PLOT 17, 0, −100   [100 points down]

5. Print square (two triangles) in main triangle, in each case:

Measure from last point	0
Without drawing	0
No dot	0
Fill triangle	80
Inverse colour	2
	82 = V

105

```
110   MOVE 250, 400
120   MOVE 350, 400                           ⎤
130   PLOT 82, −100, 100      —  useful technique
140   PLOT 82, 100, 0                          ⎦
```

6. Finish off—I'll leave you to sort out the Vs!

```
150   PLOT 0, −70, −15
160   PRINT "G"
170   PLOT 4, 280, 450
180   PRINT "B"
```

I called that "Morning Cloud" because it's a bit like a yacht (and that's the name of one). I'm sure you can take the idea further as you explore PLOT.

Here are some particularly useful PLOT Vs:

PLOT 0   Move from last point and do nothing
PLOT 4   = MOVE (from origin)
PLOT 5   = DRAW (foreground colour line from last point)
PLOT 69   Put a dot in position in foreground colour
PLOT 71   Remove a dot (= plot in background colour)

Now you can really try to understand the marvellous triangles program in the "Welcome" booklet . . . (Program A4 at the end is a posher version of that.)

POSTSCRIPT ON COLOUR

We have so far met two ways of getting coloured foregrounds and backgrounds in MODES 0–6. The first uses the COLOUR keyword, which is designed for use with text material. The second, VDU 19, applies to graphics operations (including any text).

VDU 19 . . . is rather cumbersome. It can be abbreviated a little—thus VDU 19, 1, 1; 0, 0 and VDU 19, 1, 1, 0; 0 and VDU 19, 1, 1; 0; have the same effect as the full VDU 19, 1, 1, 0, 0, 0. Hardly worth it!

There's a third colour command, GCOL (= graphics colour). GCOL 0, is followed by a number with just the same rules as the colour numbers in COLOUR statements. Thus the colour lines in Program 25 could be written like this:

```
20   GCOL 0, 130                    [yellow background]
30   GCOL 0, 1                      [red foreground]
```

This is simpler, but allows far less flexibility at our level than VDU 19. I suggest you use COLOUR statements in text-only routines, and choose between VDU 19 and GCOL 0 as you need. You will certainly prefer GCOL if you want to get more than two colours on screen at once without too much hassle.

In both cases use CLG (clear graphics area) rather than CLS (clear screen). This is particularly important if you use VDU 24 to define a graphics area within the whole screen. CLG will clear that area leaving the remaining (text) area untouched.

That reminds me that you may come across VDU 29 in this context too. It is used to change the graphics area origin coordinates from 0, 0 to X, Y.

PROJECTS

1. Make a thorough comparison of the readability of text, the contrast of colours, the clean-ness of DRAWn lines, and so on, in the different modes you have available. The best approach is to devise a simple program to run through the facilities. Take notes on your findings and refer to them during future program development.

2. Use VDU 23, MOVE, DRAW and GCOL to program a MODE 5 screen display of a house. Now add animation of, for instance, birds flying around.

3. Try to develop an illustrated child-defined story program. Start like this, perhaps:

```
50   P. "Once upon a time, there was a little boy/girl."

60   P. '' "You choose—type B or G!"

70   G$ = GET$: IF G$ < > "B"
     OR G$ < > "G" THEN 70              [picture now!!]

80   P. ' ' "What is the name of the □";

90   IF G$ = "B" THEN G$ = "boy"
     ELSE G$ = "girl"

100  P. G$ etc.                         [label picture!]
```

20 Hip Hip Array!

Well, you *can* cheer. This is the last chapter of the book and deals with lists and tables, handling which is the last remaining aspect of basic BASIC.

I've had to use arrays—the computer equivalent of lists and tables—in a couple of programs already. That's because they are *so* useful.

I'd like to illustrate the power of the concept with a program called Bar-tender, which stores the favourite drinks of a number of named people. Later versions will maybe actually pour the drinks, but for the nonce we'll leave that feature out. Here's the program concept:

1. Ask the guest's name.
2. If the name is listed, offer choice of the person's three favourite drinks.
3. Otherwise, ask for those details and store them for next time.

This is what a real bar-tender does, mentally or otherwise:

Guest	Drink 1	Drink 2	Drink 3
Mary	Small vodka	Large orange	Bitter
Mohammed	Iced Lemon	Iced tonic	Iced water
Margaret	Large neat whisky	Large neat whisky	Large neat whisky

and so on. He or she builds up a table of four columns and perhaps twenty or thirty lines (rows).

BASIC micros do the same. First however you must tell them the memory requirement. This uses a DIM (= dimension) statement. In this particular case we have a string array of, say, thirty rows and four columns. My program will start, therefore, with DIM DRINK$ (30, 4). In use, the input name (NAME$) must be tested against the first entry in each row until a match is found. Then we can go to a DRINK procedure. If there's no match, we'll need to go to an ORDER procedure.

The loop is the way to do the checking. That is straightforward because each *element* in the array carries a number (its *subscript*). The way the memory allocation looks (to humans) is shown in Figure 20.1. (In fact, in the Beeb, the subscripts start at $\emptyset$, but this is not important to us.)

Here's the program. I'll go through it afterwards, as necessary, but check the comments alongside as you think about it.

Program 26: Bar-tender

```
10   DIM DRINK$ (30, 4)              [set up array]
20   MODE 6: COLOUR 129: COLOUR 0:
     CLS                            [no room for MODE 5]
```

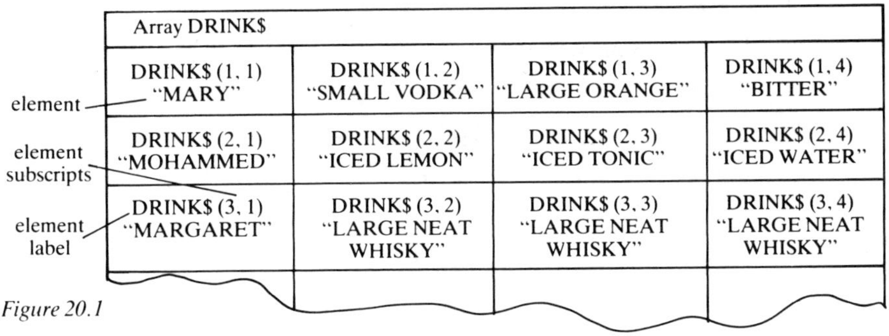

Array DRINK$			
DRINK$ (1, 1) "MARY"	DRINK$ (1, 2) "SMALL VODKA"	DRINK$ (1, 3) "LARGE ORANGE"	DRINK$ (1, 4) "BITTER"
DRINK$ (2, 1) "MOHAMMED"	DRINK$ (2, 2) "ICED LEMON"	DRINK$ (2, 3) "ICED TONIC"	DRINK$ (2, 4) "ICED WATER"
DRINK$ (3, 1) "MARGARET"	DRINK$ (3, 2) "LARGE NEAT WHISKY"	DRINK$ (3, 3) "LARGE NEAT WHISKY"	DRINK$ (3, 4) "LARGE NEAT WHISKY"

element — (points to DRINK$ (1, 1) "MARY")
element subscripts — (points to DRINK$ (2, 1))
element label — (points to DRINK$ (3, 1))

Figure 20.1

```
30   PRINT ' "□ Hallo; my name is George."
40   PRINT ' ' ' "□ Please tell me YOUR
     name." ' ' ': INPUT NAME$:
     IF LEN(NAME$) < 2 THEN 40                    [mug trap]
50   REPEAT: CLS: PRINT ' ' ' "My eyes are
     bad." ' "Are you male (M) or female
     (F)?": INPUT ' SEX$: UNTIL SEX$ =
     "M" OR SEX$ = "F"                            [mug trap]
60   CLS: PRINT ' "Thank-you, □";: IF SEX$
     = "M" SEX$ = "Sir." ELSE SEX$ =
     "Madam."
70   PRINT SEX$
80   FOR ELEMENT = 1 TO 30                        [start search loop]
90   IF DRINK$ (ELEMENT, 1) = NAME$
     THEN PROCDRINK: ELEMENT = 30:
     GOTO 120                                     [found name]
100  IF DRINK$ (ELEMENT, 1) = " " THEN
     PROCORDER: ELEMENT = 30                      [failed]
110  NEXT                                         [end loop]
120  G = GET: GOTO 20                             [next, please]
130  DEF PROCDRINK                                [choice procedure]
140  PRINT ' "□ Here are your favourite
     drinks. Please press 1, 2 or 3 to choose."
150  FOR CHOICE = 1 TO 3: PRINT '
     CHOICE; "□□"; DRINK$ (ELEMENT,
     CHOICE + 1): NEXT CHOICE                     [mini-loop]
160  G = GET − 48: IF G < 1 OR G > 3 THEN
     160                                          [mug trap]
170  CLS: PRINT ' ' "Right, □"; SEX$ '
     DRINK$ (ELEMENT, G + 1); "□ it is."
     ' ' ' ' "I'll tell the waiter.": SOUND 0,
     −15, 0, 20                                   [buzz!]
```

109

```
180   ENDPROC
190   DEF PROCORDER                          [new face procedure]
200   PRINT ' ' "I don't recall you." ' ' ' ' "Would
      you care to tell me your favourite drinks?"
210   DRINK$ (ELEMENT, 1) = NAME$            [first column]
220   FOR FAV = 1 TO 3                       [next three]
230   PRINT ' "Number □"; FAV;: INPUT
      DRINK$ (ELEMENT, FAV + 1): IF
      LEN (DRINK$ (ELEMENT, FAV + 1) )
      < 3 THEN 230                           [mug trap]
240   NEXT
250   FOR WAIT = 1 TO 3000: NEXT             [delay]
260   CLS: PROCDRINK
270   ENDPROC
```

We can see the two-dimensional DRINK$ array in four contexts here.

1. Set up with DIM, line 10. Here I've allowed for 30 guests with 3 choices each. The program will fail if more than 30 people are at your party, so modify this if you need. Use, for instance:

    ```
    5   INPUT "How many guests", N
    10  DIM DRINK$ (N, 4)
    ```

    However, note that once the program is running, you can't change the dimensions of an array. On the other hand, beware of making an array too big. Arrays use a lot of memory, which is why this program is set for MODE 6 rather than MODE 5.
2. Enter the elements of the array. You can use READ or INPUT. In Bar-tender, I used (LET), in lines 210–240. Here's the usual structure, illustrated with a one-dimensional numeric array.

    ```
    10   REM ** RAINFALL
    20   INPUT "How many months", M
    30   DIM WET (M)
    40   FOR A = 1 TO M
    50   PRINT "Rainfall for month"; M: INPUT WET (A)
    60   NEXT
    ```

3. Test the elements of the array-lines 90 and 100 above. Again a loop is often used as in this continuation of "Rainfall".

    ```
    70   FOR A = 1 TO M
    80   IF WET (A) > 1000 PRINT "Query data for month"; A
    90   NEXT
    ```

4. Print out the array elements—line 150. Or with "Rainfall"—

    ```
    100   G = GET: CLS: PRINT "Please check your data!"
    110   FOR A = 1 TO M
    ```

```
120   PRINT "Month □"; A; "□ Rainfall □"; WET (A); "□ units."
130   NEXT
140   REPEAT: PRINT ' "Any errors";: INPUT CHECK$
150   IF LEFT$(CHECK$, 1) = "Y" THEN INPUT "Month number", A:
      INPUT "Rainfall for month"; WET (A)
160   UNTIL LEFT$(CHECK$, 1) = "N"
```

Apply all those ideas to the next listing, another "Bar" program . . .

Program 27: Bar chart

```
 10   VDU 23, 224, 170, 85, 170, 85, 170, 85, 170, 85
 20   MODE 7: INPUT "Title", T$: INPUT "How many values", N
 30   DIM A (N − 1)                          [using 0 subscripts now]
 40   CLS
 50   FOR B = 1 TO N: PRINT "Value number"; B; "□";:
      INPUT A (B − 1): NEXT
 60   MODE 5: COLOUR 131: COLOUR 0: CLS
 70   FOR C = 1 TO 30
 80   FOR B = 1 TO N
 90   IF A (B − 1) < 30 − C PRINT "□"; ELSE PRINT CHR$ (224);
100   NEXT: PRINT: NEXT
110   FOR D = 1 TO N: PRINT RIGHT$(STR$ (D), 1);: NEXT: PRINT
120   FOR D = 1 TO 30: PRINT TAB (19, D − 1); RIGHT$(STR$ (30 − D), 1):
      NEXT
130   PRINT TAB (2, 5); T$: REPEAT: UNTIL FALSE
```

PROJECTS

1. An obvious use of graphics is drawing graphs. But again arrays are often relevant, so
    I kept this back until we'd done them. Study it as well as using it; check the graphics
    side as well as the array.

Program 28: Line graph

```
 10   MODE 5: COLOUR 130: COLOUR 0: CLS
 20   PRINT TAB (20);: INPUT "How many
      points", A: DIM X (A): DIM Y (A)          [arrays]
 30   CLS: PRINT "Enter x, y RETURN for each point." ' '
 40   FOR B = 1 TO A: PRINT "POINT □"; B;
      "□ X, Y:";: INPUT X (B), Y (B): NEXT      [values]
 50   CLS: FOR B = 1 TO A: PRINT; B; "X =
      □"; X (B); "□ Y = □"; Y (B): NEXT
 60   REPEAT: INPUT "Errors (Y or N)", Y$       [correct?]
 70   IF Y$ = "Y" INPUT "Which point", B: PRINT "Point □"; B;
      "□ X, Y: □";: INPUT X (B), Y (B)
```

```
 80   UNTIL Y$ = "N"
 90   PROCSCALE                              [scale up/down]
100   W = GET: GCOL 0, 130: GCOL 0, 0:
      CLG: VDU 5                             [graphics]
110   PRINT TAB (0, 29); "O"; TAB (0, 0);
      MY; TAB (20 – LEN (STR$ (MX) ), 29);
      MX                                     ["axes"]
120   MOVE X (1), Y (1)                      [start]
130   FOR B = 1 TO A – 1: PLOT 1, X (B + 1)
      – X (B), Y (B + 1) – Y (B): NEXT       [lines]
140   W = GET: GOTO 10                       [re-start]
150   DEF PROCSCALE
160   MX = 0: FOR B = 1 TO A: IF X (B) > MX MX = X (B):
      NEXT ELSE NEXT
170   MY = 0: FOR B = 1 TO A: IF Y (B) > MY MY = Y (B):
      NEXT ELSE NEXT
180   FOR B = 1 TO A: X (B) = X (B) * (1280/MX): Y (B) =
      Y (B) * (1024/MY): NEXT
190   ENDPROC
```

2. Program A12 also depends heavily on the use of arrays. It is worth studying for that alone—but also note the "sorting" concept in the middle. This is actually a fairly tough program to follow as a whole, but I hope the principles become clear. Anyway it's a *very* useful program.

3. Devise a simple directory program to hold names and phone numbers in *two* string arrays, so that you can get the 'phone number of any friend listed by entering the name. Start off with

```
10   DIM NAME$ (20) NUMBER$ (20)
```

if there are twenty records.

4. Use a similar parallel pair of one-dimension arrays to hold the names and exam marks of, say, 30 pupils. Start with:

```
10   DIM NAME$ (30) MARK (30)
```

Try to set it up so you have a menu to choose from to give such things as highest mark, lowest mark and mean; full list in name order; full list in mark order. Use procedures for these tasks.

Additional Programs

Program A1 (a): Printout

This is a very simple (but maybe useful?) program to get you used to some major programming ideas.

```
10  MODE 5
20  COLOUR 2
30  COLOUR 129
40  CLS
50  REPEAT
60  PRINT ' ' "Give me a number:"
70  INPUT NUMBER
80  LET SQUARE = NUMBER * NUMBER
90  LET CUBE = SQUARE * NUMBER
100 PRINT "□ Number: □"; NUMBER
110 PRINT "□ Square: □"; SQUARE
120 PRINT "□ Cube: □ □ □"; CUBE
130 UNTIL FALSE                        [stop with ESCAPE]
```

Program A1 (b): Bonus

As the above will seem very trivial once you've got very far into this book, here's a bonus program which I think you'll enjoy much longer! You'll also find the ideas in it, once explored, very useful in any MODE 7 routines you write.

```
10  INPUT "Message", A$                [up to 28 characters]
20  CLS
30  FOR A = 1 TO 7
40  PRINT CHR$ (136) CHR$ (A + 128), A$
50  PRINT CHR$ (136 − A) CHR$ (141) A$ ' CHR$ (136 − A)
    CHR$ (141) A$
60  NEXT
70  REPEAT: UNTIL FALSE
```

Try "messages" consisting of nice pattern-generating symbols . . .

Program A2: Train race

No way is this a novel game—two engines race across the screen, moving forward a random distance each move until one or other reaches the end.

The principle is the basis of a number of similar exercises, non-interactive or interactive. It is straightforward to add twiddly bits like reverse as well as forward motion, barriers and switching tracks (one reason I chose MODE 6, which gives you the "railway lines" for free).

```
10  VDU 23, 225, 0, 255, 65, 73, 77, 75, 127, 127  ┐
20  VDU 23, 226, 0, 0, 0, 0, 0, 0, 24, 255, 255    │
                                                    ├─ engine blocks
30  VDU 23, 227, 0, 28, 28, 28, 28, 28, 254, 254   │
40  VDU 23, 228, 127, 127, 127, 127, 255, 13, 7, 2 ┘
```

```
 50   VDU 23, 229, 255, 255, 255, 255, 255, 155, ⎤
      14, 4                                        ⎥
 60   VDU 23, 230, 254, 254, 254, 254, 255, 54,    ⎬ engine blocks
      28, 8                                        ⎦
 70   VDU 23, 231, 16, 168, 84, 170, 84, 120, 20,
      40                                              [smoke]
 80   MODE 6
 90   VDU 5
100   VDU 19, 1, 0, 0, 0, 0, 19, 0, 3, 0, 0, 0      [colour definition]
110   CLS
120   A1 = 0: A2 = 0: PRINT TAB (36, 10);
      "ME"; TAB (36, 16); "YOU"
130   REPEAT                                         [start loop]
140   A1 = A1 + RND (3): B = 9      ⎤
                                    ⎬ train 1
150   PROCT (A1, B)                 ⎦
160   A2 = A2 + RND (3): B = 15     ⎤
                                    ⎬ train 2
170   PROCT (A2, B)                 ⎦
180   UNTIL A1 > 26 OR A2 > 26                       [end loop]
190   PRINT TAB (2, 20);
200   IF A1 > 26 THEN PRINT "My"; ELSE
      PRINT "Your";
210   PRINT " train won!"
220   FOR Z = 1 TO 3000: NEXT                        [pause]
230   GOTO 110                                       [re-start]
240   DEF PROCT (A, B)
250   PRINT TAB (A + 4, B); CHR$ (231):
      SOUND 1, − 15, B ∗ 4, 4                        [smoke, whistle]
260   PRINT TAB (A, B + 1); "□ □ □" +         ⎤
      CHR$ (225) + CHR$ (226) + CHR$ (227);   ⎥
      TAB (A, B + 2); "□ □ □" +CHR$ (228)+    ⎬ engine
      CHR$ (229) + CHR$ (230)                  ⎦
270   FOR Z = 1 TO 1000: NEXT                        [pause]
280   ENDPROC
```

Program A3: Sketch pad

This program allows you to build up a "picture" using any keyboard character within the MODE 5 "canvas". You can make it as sophisticated as you wish, but already the user instructions need thought. Here they are:

1. If an inverse "?" is on screen, whatever character you enter except "S" will appear at that position. If you enter "S" the program stops.
2. If there is no inverse "?" enter "U", "D", "L", or "R" to move the "cursor" up, down, left or right (unless it's at the edge of the screen).

116

```
10    MODE 5: COLOUR 129: COLOUR 3: CLS
20    VDU 23, 225, 193, 221, 253, 225, 239, 239, 255, 239
30    X = 10: Y = 15                        [start at centre]
40    PRINT TAB (X, Y); CHR$ (225)
50    A$ = GET$: IF A$ = " " THEN 50
60    IF A$ = "S" THEN 140
70    PRINT TAB (X, Y); A$
80    A$ = GET$: IF A$ = " " THEN 80
90    IF A$ = "U" AND Y − 1 > = 1 THEN Y = Y− 1: GOTO 40
100   IF A$ = "D" AND Y + 1 < = 28 THEN Y = Y + 1: GOTO 40
110   IF A$ = "R" AND X + 1 < = 18 THEN X = X + 1: GOTO 40
120   IF A$ = "L" AND X − 1 > = 1 THEN X = X − 1: GOTO 40
130   GOTO 80
140   REPEAT: UNTIL FALSE
```

Program A4: Wallpaper

Many people reckon that the little four-line program on page 9 is the most delightful thing in the whole "Welcome" package. You may just about recognize it towards the end of this impress-your-visitors-with-the-BBC program. It's not deep, but it includes some nice effects.

```
10    MODE 5: COLOUR 2: COLOUR 129: CLS
20    PRINT TAB (2, 3); "What is your name";: INPUT N$
30    COLOUR 1: COLOUR 130: CLS            [change colours]
40    PRINT TAB (1, 3); "Thanks, □"; N$; "."
50    G = INKEY (500)
60    VDU 19, 1, 0, 0, 0                    [change foreground]
70    REPEAT
80    PRINT ' ' TAB (1); "Give me a number", "between 1 and 10."
90    B = 1
100   *FX 15, 0                             [clear INPUT buffer]
110   B = INKEY (400) − 48: PROCCHIME       [accept number in 4s]
120   UNTIL B < 2 OR B > 9                  [leave loop]
130   CLS
140   FOR A = 1 TO 400: PRINT N$; "□";:
      NEXT                                  [name pattern]
150   C = 7
160   VDU 19, 1, C, 0, 0: CLS              [background colour]
170   FOR A = 1 TO 100:
      GCOL RND (3), RND (7)                 [random foreground]
180   PLOT 85, RND (1280), RND (1024)       [random triangle]
```

117

```
190   SOUND A, A, A, A: FOR B = 1 TO
      1000: NEXT                          ["concrete music"]
200   NEXT
210   C = C − 1: IF C = −1 THEN 10        [re-start]
220   GOTO 160
230   DEF PROCCHIME
240   FOR C = 1 TO B: FOR A = 15 TO 25: SOUND 1, A, 40, 6
250   NEXT: NEXT: FOR C = 1 TO 4000: NEXT: ENDPROC
```

Program A5: Reflex timer

```
10    REPEAT: MODE 5: COLOUR 130: COLOUR 0: CLS
20    PRINT TAB (20); "REFLEX TIMER" ' "============="
30    PRINT ' ' ' "Enter number of your choice:" ' ' "□ 1. Simple: screen"
      ' ' "□ 2. Harder: sound" ' ' "□ 3. Harder: both"
40    L = ASC (INKEY$ (3E4) ) − 48: IF L < 0
      OR L > 3 GOTO 40                     [mug trap]
50    CLS: TB = 1000: SUM = 0:
      GOSUB L * 100: UNTIL FALSE           [computed]
100   FOR A = 1 TO 10: CLS: PRINT ' ' "TEST 1□" ' ' "GO □ □ □"; A
110   TIME = 0: REPEAT: UNTIL TIME
      > 100                                [delay]
120   PRINT ' ' ' "Press RETURN key" ' "when screen blanks!"
130   PROCTIME1                           [random delay]
140   CLS
150   PROCTIME2                           [start timing]
160   NEXT: RETURN
200   FOR A = 1 TO 10: CLS: PRINT ' ' "TEST 2" ' ' "GO □ □"; A
210   TIME = 0: REPEAT: UNTIL TIME > 100
220   PRINT ' ' ' "Press RETURN key" ' "when buzzer buzzes!"
230   PROCTIME1
240   SOUND 0, −15, 2, 2                  [short buzz]
250   PROCTIME2
260   NEXT: RETURN
300   FOR A = 1 TO 10: CLS: PRINT ' ' "TEST 3" ' ' "GO □ □ □"; A
310   TIME = 0: REPEAT: UNTIL TIME > 100
320   PRINT ' "Press RETURN key" ' "when buzzer buzzes" '
      "after screen clears!"
330   PROCTIME1: SOUND 0, −15, 2, 2: PROCTIME1: CLS: PROCTIME1:
      SOUND 0, −15, 2, 2
```

```
340   PROCTIME2.
350   NEXT: RETURN
400   DEF PROCTIME1
410   FOR B = 1 TO 500 + RND (10000):
      NEXT                                    [random delay]
420   ENDPROC
450   DEF PROCTIME2
460   TIME = 10: *FX 15, 1                     [cheat reduce]
470   L = INKEY (3E4): T = TIME / 100          [reaction time]
480   SUM = SUM + T: TM = SUM/A:
      IF T < TB   TB = T                       [evaluate]
490   PROCREFLEX                               [nesting!]
500   PRINT ' ' ' "RETURN to go on":
      INPUT B                                  [to next go]
510   ENDPROC
550   DEF PROCREFLEX
560   PRINT ' ' ' "Result: □"; T; " sec"
570   PRINT ' ' ' "Best: □ □ □"; TB; " sec"
580   PRINT ' ' ' "Mean: □ □ □"; INT (100 * TM + .5) / 100; "sec"
590   PRINT ' ' ' "Go □"; A
600   ENDPROC
```

Program A6: Guess the hard number

This is a much posher version of Program 1, with three levels of difficulty, and as a result, just about the most complex numerical expression I've ever writen (line 110). That uses logical sub-expressions as factors. The rest is fairly straightforward to make up for it!

```
10    MODE 5: COLOUR 129: COLOUR 3: CLS
20    REC = 100: LIM = 99                      (you may change LIMit if
                                               you want]
30    REPEAT
40    CLS: GUESS = 0: PRINT TAB (24); "NUMBER GUESS"; TAB (4);
      "= = = = = = = = = = = ="; TAB (0, 10); "Please type name" ' '
      "□ (with RETURN)" ' '
50    INPUT N$
60    PRINT ' ' "Thank-you,"; N$; "."
70    INPUT ' ' "Level (1, 2 or 3)", L
80    IF L < 1 OR L > 3 GOTO 70
90    FOR A = 1 TO 2000: NEXT
100   CLS: GUESS = 0
```

```
110   Z = RND (1): X = (RND (LIM) * ( − (L = 1) ) ) + ( (1 + (INT
      (RND (1) * LIM * 10) ) / 10) * (− (L = 2) ) ) + ( (1 + (INT (RND (1)
      * LIM * 10) ) / 10) * ( (−1 * (Z > .5)
      + (Z < = .5) ) * (L = 3) ) )                              [phew]
120   PRINT ' "I am thinking of a number up to □"; LIM + 1; ".": REPEAT
130   PRINT ' "PLEASE ENTER GUESS."
140   INPUT Y: GUESS = GUESS + 1
150   IF Y < X PRINT "Too low . . ." ELSE IF Y > X PRINT "Too high . . ."
      ELSE PRINT "Right!"
160   UNTIL Y = X
170   PRINT ' ' ' "Got it in □"; GUESS; "!"
180   IF GUESS < REC PRINT ' "□ A RECORD!!!": REC = GUESS:
      REC$ = N$: RECL = L
190   FOR A = 1 TO 8000: NEXT: CLS
200   PRINT ' ' ' "Best score so far: □", , REC ' ' "Scored by □"; REC$ '
      "Level □"; RECL
210   FOR A = 1 TO 2000: NEXT
220   PRINT ' ' ' "Press RETURN to try again."       [choice if you prefer]
230   INPUT S$: GOTO 40: UNTIL FALSE
```

Program A7: Hangman

This got longer than I hoped—and better than I expected. You may wish to improve the user-defined graphics—but I've seen far less realistic hangmen programs!

```
10    VDU 23, 224, 255, 255, 255, 255, 255, 255, 255, 255     [black square]
20    VDU 23, 225, 255, 255, 255, 255, 129, 255, 255, 255     [inverse dash]
30    VDU 23, 226, 13, 11, 13, 11, 13, 11, 13, 11
40    VDU 23, 227, 176, 208, 176, 208, 176, 208, 176, 208  ⌉
50    VDU 23, 228, 0, 0, 1, 3, 3, 3, 7, 7                   |
60    VDU 23, 229, 0, 170, 255, 221, 136, 255, 247, 247     |
70    VDU 23, 230, 0, 128, 192, 224, 224, 224, 240, 240     |
80    VDU 23, 231, 7, 7, 3, 1, 1, 1, 0, 0                   ├─ head (a big one!)
90    VDU 23, 232, 227, 255, 255, 193, 193, 255, 255, 255   |
100   VDU 23, 233, 240, 240, 224, 192, 192, 192, 128, 0     ⌋
110   MODE 5: COLOUR 129: COLOUR 0: CLS
120   FOR A = 1 TO 6                                      [question]
130   READ Q$: L = LEN Q$: OK = 0: NO = 0:
      GO = 0: U$ = "□"
140   PROCDASH
```

120

```
150    REPEAT                                          [start guessing]
160    PRINT TAB (2, 1); "Used:"; U$; TAB (2, 27);
       "Enter letter": G = GET: PROCTEST:
       IF F THEN 160                                   [mug traps]
170    GO = GO + 1: PROCCHECK
180    UNTIL OK = L OR NO = 8                          [succeed or fail]
190    PRINT TAB (2, 27); "[12 spaces]": TIME = 0:
       REPEAT: UNTIL TIME > 750: CLS: NEXT: STOP
500    DATA STRENGTH, WEAKNESS, PROGRAM,
       HANGPERSON, BBC, BYEBYE
510    DEF PROCDASH                                    [dash word]
520    PRINT TAB (2, 10); STRING$ (L, CHR$ (225) ):
       ENDPROC
550    DEF PROCTEST                                    [input checks]
560    G$ = CHR$ (G)                                   [convert to string]
570    F = 0: IF G < 65 OR G > 90 F = 1: ENDPROC
580    IF INSTR (U$, G$) > 0 F = 1: ENDPROC
590    U$ = U$ + G$: ENDPROC
600    DEF PROCCHECK                                   [yes or no?]
610    F = 0: FOR B = 1 TO L:
       IF G$ = MID$(Q$, B, 1) PROCOK                   [good guess]
620    NEXT: IF F = 0 PROCNO                           [bad one]
630    ENDPROC
650    DEF PROCOK
660    OK = OK + 1: F = 1: PRINT TAB (B + 1, 10); G$: ENDPROC
700    DEF PROCNO
710    NO = NO + 1: GOSUB (1000 + NO * 50):
       ENDPROC                                         [to gallows]
1050   PRINT TAB (10, 25); STRING$ (9, CHR$ (224) ): RETURN
1100   FOR C = 24 TO 2 STEP −1: PRINT TAB (14, C); CHR$ (224):
       NEXT: RETURN
1150   FOR C = 14 TO 10 STEP −1: PRINT TAB (C, 2); CHR$ (224):
       NEXT: RETURN
1200   FOR C = 3 TO 13: PRINT TAB (11, C); ".": NEXT: RETURN
1250   FOR C = 21 TO 24: PRINT TAB (10, C); CHR$ (226) + "□"
       + CHR$ (227): NEXT: RETURN
1300   FOR C = 18 TO 20: PRINT TAB (9, C); CHR$ (226) + CHR$ (226)
       + CHR$ (224) + CHR$ (227) + CHR$ (227): NEXT: PRINT TAB (9, 17);
       CHR$ (226) + STRING$ (3, CHR$ (224) ) + CHR$ (227): RETURN
```

1350 PRINT TAB (10, 14); CHR$ (228) + CHR$ (229) + CHR$ (230)
      + CHR$ (10) + STRING$ (3, CHR$ (8)) + CHR$ (231) + CHR$ (232)
      + CHR$ (233); TAB (11, 16); CHR$ (224): RETURN

1400 PRINT TAB (4, 25); "HANGED [5 spaces]"; TAB (2, 10); Q$: RETURN

Program A8: Tables test

A sophisticated menu-driven version of a standard "teaching" program. Hope you like the menu!

```
 10  VDU 23, 224, 255, 170, 170, 170, 170, 170, 128, 193
 20  VDU 23, 225, 247, 247, 247, 247, 247, 247, 247, 255
 30  VDU 23, 226, 255, 247, 231, 231, 231, 231, 231, 231
 40  M$ = CHR$ (224) + CHR$ (226) + CHR$ (10) + CHR$ (8) + CHR$ (8)
     + CHR$ (225) + CHR$ (225)
 50  MODE 5: COLOUR 129: COLOUR 0
 60  REPEAT: CLS
 70  PRINT TAB (3, 2); M$; TAB (7, 3); "MENU"; TAB (7, 4); "====";
     TAB (13, 2); M$
 80  PRINT ' ' ' "1. Show table and □ □ □ test" ' ' "2. Test, no show" ' '
     "3. Test on 2–5" ' ' "4. Test on 6–12" ' ' "5. Test on 2–12"
 90  FOR A = 1 TO 2000: NEXT
100  PRINT ' ' ' "Enter number of your choice" ' ' ' '
110  *FX 15, 0                              [clear input buffer memory]
120  L = INKEY (3E4) − 48                   [long wait for choice]
130  IF L < 1 OR L > 5 GOTO 110             [full mug trap]
140  F1 = −(L=1): F2 = −(L=2): F3 = − (L=3): F4 = −(L=4): F5 = −(L=5)
150  IF F1 OR F2 INPUT ' ' "Which table", T: IF T < 2 OR T > 12 GOTO 150
160  IF F1 PROCTABLE
170  SCORE = 0: FOR Q = 1 TO 10
180  S = 1 + RND (11): IF F3 T = 1 + RND (4) ELSE IF F4 T = 5 + RND (7)
     ELSE IF F5 T = 1 + RND (11)            [choice of questions]
190  PRINT ' "Question "; Q; "What is □"; S; "□times□"; T; "?",: INPUT R
200  IF R = S * T PRINT, "Yes": SCORE = SCORE + 1 ELSE PRINT "No"
210  NEXT
220  PRINT ' ' ' "Your SCORE is□"; SCORE: FOR A = 1 TO 10000: NEXT:
     UNTIL FALSE
230  DEF PROCTABLE
240  FOR A = 1 TO 12: PRINT ';: IF A < 10 PRINT "□";
250  PRINT; A; "□times□"; T; "□is□"; A * T: NEXT
260  ENDPROC
```

Program A9: Target practice

In each run you have ten attempts to hit the target with a shot from a gun the other side of a barrier. The routine in lines 220–250 plots the parabolic trajectory (you could add lines to bring in air friction and wind if you wish). For each run, gun and target are placed at random and the barrier has random height and width.

```
 10   VDU 23, 225, 3, 6, 60, 40, 104, 60, 126, 255
 20   VDU 23, 226, 36, 90, 165, 90, 60, 155, 24, 60
 30   VDU 23, 227, 24, 36, 66, 153, 153, 66, 36, 127
 40   VDU 23, 228, 28, 42, 85, 170, 127, 170, 85, 255
 50   MODE 5                                              [set up playing area]
 60   GCOL 0, 130
 70   GCOL 0, 0
 80   VDU 5
 90   CLG
100   A = RND (4) − 1                                     [set up random sites]
110   B = RND (4) + 15
120   C = RND (9) + 1
130   D = 0                                               [go count]
140   REPEAT                                              [go loop]
150   D = D + 1
160   PROCG                                               [set up characters]
170   MOVE 10, 976: INPUT "Angle", A1
180   MOVE 10, 936: INPUT "Speed", E
190   AN = A1 * PI / 180                                  [convert to radians]
200   X = 8
210   REPEAT                                              [trajectory loop]
220   X1 = X + 64 * (A + 1)
230   Y = 32 + X * TAN (AN) − X↑2 / (E↑2 * COS (AN)↑2)
240   PLOT 69, X1, Y + 32: SOUND 1, −10, Y/5 + 20, 2
250   X = X + 16
260   UNTIL X > 1280 OR Y < = 32 OR
      POINT (X1 + 9, Y + 32) = 0                          [end trajectory cases]
270   PRINT CHR$ (226): SOUND 0, −15, 6, 20               [detonate]
280   FOR F = 1 TO 1E4: NEXT                              [delay]
290   CLG
300   UNTIL D = 10 OR ABS (X1 − B * 64) < 40              [end go cases]
310   IF D = 10 THEN PRINT TAB (4, 10); "USELESS"
      ELSE PRINT TAB (4, 10); "GOOD SHOT!" ' ' "□ □
      You got it in"; D; "."
320   FOR F = 1 TO 1E4: NEXT
```

330 PRINT ' ' "HAVE ANOTHER GO . . .":

GOTO 90   [re-start]

340 DEF PROCG

350 LOCAL D

360 PRINT TAB (A, 30); CHR$ (225)   [gun]

370 PRINT TAB (B, 30); CHR$ (227)   [target]

380 FOR D = 1 TO C: PRINT TAB (5, 30 − D + 1);

STRING$ (C, CHR$ (228)): NEXT   [barrier]

390 ENDPROC

Program A10: Guess the word

This is rather an intriguing word game, that requires a fair amount of thought. At each attempt, you must enter a word of the right length (the display shows how many letters there are). The computer's response is, as one may expect, to replace dashes by correct letters in the correct places. For an incorrect letter, the display turns to an inverse ">" if the guess is earlier in the alphabet than the correct letter; inverse "<" indicates that your letter is later in the alphabet than it should be. The DATA in line 310 may of course be altered at will.

```
10   MODE 5

20   COLOUR 130

30   COLOUR 1

40   VDU 23, 224, 85, 170, 85, 170, 85, 170, 85, 170    [a useful character, this!]

50   VDU 23, 225, 255, 255, 255, 255, 129, 255, 255, 255    [inverse dash]

60   VDU 23, 226, 251, 247, 239, 223, 191, 223, 239, 247    [inverse <]

70   VDU 23, 227, 191, 223, 239, 247, 251, 247, 239, 223    [inverse >]

80   C$ = "[20 spaces]"

90   B$ = CHR$ (224)

100  A$ = STRING$ (16, B$) + CHR$ (10) + STRING$ (16, CHR$ (8) ) +
     B$ + "GUESS THE WORD" + B$ + CHR$ (10) +
     STRING$ (16, CHR$ (8) ) + STRING$ (16, B$)

110  WORD = 0

120  REPEAT

130  WORD = WORD + 1

140  GO = 0

150  CLS

160  PRINT TAB (22); A$

170  READ X$: L = LEN X$

180  FOR B = 1 TO L: PRINT TAB (B + 2, 10); CHR$ (225): NEXT

190  REPEAT: CHECK = 0

200  PRINT TAB (0, 14); "Enter guess & RETURN"

210  INPUT B$: GO = GO + 1

220  IF LEN B$ < > L PRINT "Wrong length; again.": GOTO 210
```

124

```
230   FOR B = 1 TO L: IF MID$(B$, B, 1) < MID$(X$, B, 1) PRINT TAB
      (B + 2, 1Ø); CHR$ (227) ELSE IF MID$(B$, B, 1) > MID$(X$, B, 1)
      PRINT TAB (B+ 2, 1Ø); CHR$ (226) ELSE PRINT TAB (B + 2, 1Ø);
      MID$(X$, B, 1): CHECK = CHECK + 1

240   NEXT: PRINT ' ' ' ' ' ' C$, C$

250   UNTIL CHECK = L

260   PRINT ' ' ' C$ ' ' ' "Got it—"; GO; "□goes."

270   IF WORD = 6 THEN FOR B = 1 TO 4ØØØ: NEXT: CLS:
      PRINT TAB (2, 12); "Well, time's up." ' ' ' ' ' ': END

280   PRINT TAB (2, 3Ø);: INPUT "Again (Y or N)", Y$

290   UNTIL Y$ < > "Y"

3ØØ   CLS: PRINT TAB (2, 12); "That's it, then." ' ' ' ' ' ': END

31Ø   DATA MADAM, BEEB, SPECTRUM, ZEBRA, BUZZ, COMPUTER
```

Program A11: Lunarvader

As the name indicates, this is a cross between "lunar lander" and "space invader". I'll
leave you to work out what to do . . .

```
1Ø   VDU 23, 224, 4, 7, 15, 31, 57, 57, 63, 126

2Ø   VDU 23, 225, 32, 224, 24Ø, 248, 156, 156, 252, 126

3Ø   VDU 23, 226, 255, 63, 39, 37, 36, 36, 36, 1Ø8

4Ø   VDU 23, 227, 255, 252, 228, 164, 36, 36, 36, 54

5Ø   VDU 23, 228, 1, 1, 1, 1, 1, 1, 1, 1

6Ø   CLS

7Ø   INPUT "What level (Ø: easy—19: awful)", L

8Ø   PRINT TAB (Ø, 1Ø); "Z: move left; /: move right"

9Ø   X$ = INKEY$ (5ØØ)                      [delay]

1ØØ  *FX 15                                 [clear keyboard buffer]

11Ø  MODE 5: GCOL Ø, 13Ø: VDU 5: GCOL Ø, 1: CLG

12Ø  S = RND (1ØØØ + L * 5) + 1ØØ: PROCP    [call procedure P]

13Ø  X = RND (115Ø + L * 5): Y = 1ØØØ: A = 1

14Ø  REPEAT: CLS: PROCP: PROCC              [call procedures]

15Ø  X$ = INKEY$ (96 − L * 5)               [varies speed]

16Ø  IF X$ = "Z" AND X > 5Ø − L * 5 THEN X = X − (15 − A) * 1Ø

17Ø  IF X$ = "/" AND X < 12ØØ + L * 5 THEN X = X + (15 − A) * 1Ø

18Ø  A = A + 1: Y = Y − 7Ø

19Ø  UNTIL A = 15                           [end loop]

2ØØ  MOVE 1ØØ, 6ØØ: IF ABS (S − X) < 7 THEN PRINT
     "SPLAT" ELSE IF ABS (S − X) < 15 THEN PRINT
     "KEEP TRYING" ELSE PRINT "USELESS"     [change print position]

21Ø  FOR B = 1 TO 25ØØ − L * 1ØØ: NEXT:
     GOTO 1ØØ                               [re-start]
```

```
220   DEF PROCP
230   MOVE S, 32
240   PRINT CHR$ (228) + CHR$ (8) + CHR$ (10) + CHR$ (228)
250   ENDPROC
260   DEF PROCC
270   MOVE X, Y: PRINT CHR$ (224) + CHR$ (225)
280   MOVE X, Y − 32: PRINT CHR$ (226) + CHR$ (227)
290   SOUND 0, −A, A * 15, A
300   ENDPROC
```

Program A12: Big print sums

As I am a teacher, I hope you'll forgive my making the last program in the book specifically one for teachers. As it stands it stores a set of sums in DATA (lines 120 on); each is then displayed as three lines in big print characters, line by line (PROCMAG). You should be able to adapt it to your own needs, including scrolling. However in Model A modes you are restricted to five characters per line.

```
 10   MODE 6
 20   VDU 23, 225, 170, 85, 170, 85, 170, 85, 170, 85       [experiment with this!]
 30   CLS: READ A$: IF A$ = "END" THEN 110
 40   PROCBLANK
 50   FOR A = 1 TO 16 STEP 8                                 [three lines]
 60   B$ = MID$(B$, A/8 * 5 + 1, 5)                          [select sub-string]
 70   PROCMAG
 80   G = GET                                                [wait for (R)]
 90   NEXT
100   GOTO 30                                                [next sum]
110   STOP
120   DATA "10000 / □ 250 = □ □ 40"
130   DATA "□ □ 234 + □ □ 47 = □ 281"                        [etc.]
140   DATAEND                                               [no more]
150   DEF PROCBLANK                                         [makes A$ up to 15]
160   IF LEN (A$) < 15 THEN A$ = A$ + STRING$ (15 − LEN (A$), "□")
170   ENDPROC
180   DEF PROCMAG: LOCAL X, Y
190   FOR Y = 0 TO 7: PRINT TAB (0, A + Y)
200   FOR B = 1 TO 5
210   C$ = MID$(B$, B, 1)                                    [select character]
220   C = ? ( ( (ASC (C$) − 32) * 8 + &C000 + Y)            [get code from ROM]
230   FOR X = 7 TO 0 STEP −1
240   IF (C AND (2 ↑ X) ) = 2 ↑ X PRINT CHR$ (225); ELSE PRINT "□";
250   NEXT: NEXT: NEXT
260   ENDPROC
```

Index

Note: The numbers refer to chapters and *not* to pages.

Other titles of interest

Further Programming for the BBC Micro
Alan Thomas

PEEK, POKE, BYTE & RAM! Basic Programming for the ZX81
Ian Stewart & Robin Jones

'Far and away the best book for ZX81 users new to computing'—*Popular Computing Weekly*

'. . . the best introduction to using this trail-blazing micro'—*Computers in Schools*

'One of fifty books already published on the Sinclair micros, it is the best introduction accessible to all computing novices'—*Laboratory Equipment Digest*

Machine Code and better Basic
Ian Stewart & Robin Jones

The ZX81 Add-On Book
Martin Wren-Hilton

Easy Programming for the ZX Spectrum
Ian Stewart & Robin Jones

ComputerPuzzles: For Spectrum and ZX81
Ian Stewart & Robin Jones

Games to Play on Your ZX Spectrum
Martin Wren-Hilton

Available from January '83

Spectrum in Education
Eric Deeson

Further Programming for the ZX Spectrum
Ian Stewart & Robin Jones

Spectrum Machine Code
Ian Stewart & Robin Jones

Brainteasers for BASIC Computers
Gordon Lee

Shiva Software

Spectrum Special 1
Ian Stewart & Robin Jones

A selection of 10 educational games and puzzles.

Plus more to come!